How to Really Watch

The Godfather

By Jane Cavolina Meara

Growing Up Catholic
More Growing Up Catholic

HOW TO REALLY WATCH

The Godfather

Capos, Cannolis, Consiglieres, and the Truth About the Corleones

Ellen Cavolina and Jane Cavolina Meara

St. Martin's Press   New York

Design by Jaye Zimet

Library of Congress Cataloging-in-Publication Data

Cavolina, Ellen.
    How to really watch the Godfather : Capos, Cannolis, Consiglieres, and the truth about the Corleones / Ellen Cavolina and Jane Cavolina Meara.
        p.   cm.
    ISBN 0-312-06323-7
    1. Italian Americans—United States—Humor. 2. Godfather (Motion picture)—Humor. I. Meara, Mary Jane Frances Cavolina.
II. Title.
PN6231.I85C38   1991
305.85'1073'0207—dc20   91-21003
                                                                CIP

First Edition

10 9 8 7 6 5 4 3 2 1

*To Lisa Cavolina and Brian Meara, who made us watch this
movie until we got it*

*To our parents, Shirley and Frank Cavolina, who gave us
their vision of life and family as things powerful and deep*

*To Bella Rodriguez, for years of tender loving care, and for
teaching us how to appreciate the movies*

And to the whole Cavolina family

Acknowledgments

To Mario Puzo, for inventing this wonderful family, and to Francis Ford Coppola for bringing them so dramatically to life. We thank them both.

To the late Carmine Coppola, for a magnificent and moving score.

To Elaine Markson, who was enthusiastic right from the start, and who, with Lisa Callamaro and Karin Beisch, worked tirelessly in our behalf. We thank them sincerely.

To Jim Fitzgerald, who had confidence in our obsession, Alex Kuczynski, for her hard work and attention, and to Jaye Zimet for making a beautiful book.

To Lesley Jones and Terry Nolan, for their love and support; to Alison de Metz and Peter Lydon, who were there when this book began; and to all our dear, dear friends in England.

To Doug and Susan Cassidy for their warmth and quiet encouragement. To each and every Cavolina—Robert, who takes great pride in all we do; Larry, Lorraine, Jason and Jessica, for their phone calls and their computer; Lisa, the real Connie; Michael (who reported in first on *Godfather III*), Joan Krista, Julie and Jeremy, for their excitement; and Mom and Dad, for straightening out a million details in the book, just like our lives.

Ellen Cavolina would like to acknowledge warmly the following people:

Dr. Katharine Weiser, for being so supportive and so dear for so long.

John Vitagliano for warm, inexhaustible comraderie.

Christopher Brescia for his tenderness and moral support.

Andrea Kabas for tirelessly caring about every detail of the book and my life.

Prof. Robert J. White for so generously sharing his joy of life and learning with me.

Michelle Dubuc and Michael Gleason for all their big and little kindnesses to me and their sense of humor.

Tracy Kohlman, the stand-up proofreader, for her enthusiasm and laughter.

Marc Mowrey, fellow tenderfoot, for his generosity of spirit and warm good humor throughout.

Theresa Brockett—whose pulsing light of life can never be extinguished—for encouraging and motivating me to attain my heart's desire.

Jane Cavolina Meara would like to thank:

Betty Prashker, Erica Marcus, Christine Pilla, and all her friends at Crown for their generous enthusiasm and warm support.

All the Mearas, especially Charlie and Ethel, who are always there for me.

Jeff Stone, a true and valued friend.

Richard Pine, for his unflagging encouragement.

Larry Goldman, for his generous and invaluable help.

Rocky and CNN, who kept us company.

The dear memory of Howard Cady, a great man and a great editor, who is still with those who love him.

Contents

Chapter One

Spending the Day with the Corleones

From Casa Nostra to Casa Vostra
We cordially invite you to join us in spending a day
with the Corleone family.

There will be lots of food, lots of music, lots of
exciting company. You'll experience the drama of
Shakespeare, the beauty of opera, and the
poignancy of real life.

Date: December 7

Place: The Mall, Long Beach

Time: All Day

RSVP: Long Beach 4-5620

☞ How to Throw a Godfather Party

The best way to watch *The Godfather* is in the company of like-minded fanatics, close friends and relations, and people who know a beautiful thing when they see one. Do not watch it with people who say things like, "This movie is too violent," or "I like Kay." They are not simpatico. Add enough food for an army, good Italian wine, some pastry, comfortable seating and presto, you have a Godfather party.

Here are the necessary ingredients for a Godfather party *con gusto:*

1. Assembling the Right Crowd

The right crowd is anyone you have a real understanding with. This is not a party for everybody. It's not just about inviting people that you like; like is not enough. You want special people, people who feel the same way you do about the Godfather or have the potential to.

When you make your list, family members should be at the top—close or not, there is a strong connection. Family is irrefutably, undeniably there. It doesn't really matter if you get along; blood is what matters. An occasional fight might add to the authenticity. And you might find yourself a good "Sonny". (SEE BELOW)

Close friends are as good as family, but different. They do not have to be Italian. They do not have to be Catholic. They don't have to be anything but people you can relate to. Friends who *gabeesh* won't say "half of this movie is in another language," and other irritating things; they will be transported along with you.

Assess your possible guest list carefully. The wrong guest can ruin a Godfather party, but keep an open mind. There is a Godfather lover lurking in the soul of every sensitive person. You may end up with a few converts.

2. Assigning appropriate parts to your guests

Part of the job of being Godfather host is contemplating role assignments. You have to start to think about this before the party.

After you've watched the movie several times, you'll see similarities between certain people you know and characters in *The Godfather*. Be sure to have these people at your party. They will help bring the movie out of the TV set and into the living room. If you are right about your characterizations, your guests will accept their role assignments enthusiastically, recognizing in themselves the Connie that's been smoldering for years or the barely concealed Willi Cicci (pronounced *Cheech*). Sometimes guests will claim sympathy with unlikely characters for reasons that are not apparent to you, and will lapse into their roles at the drop of a meatball. Your mother may feel like Sonny inside. Let her. And, God forbid, someone you love may feel like Kay. It's a free country. Expression like this should be encouraged.

Who plays who should be open to discussion. (As with any gathering of Italians and/or pseudo-Italians, discussion is a little louder than with other folks. This is okay.) People should not be confined to characters of their age or their sex or their looks; anybody can be anybody. But not just anybody can be Michael.

He is chosen by consensus, if at all.

There are some characters in *The Godfather* that people are not going to want to play. There are small roles (Enzo the baker), dirty roles (Sonny's bimbo), mean roles (Carlo), and sleazy roles (Senator Geary from Nevada). Even though people may want only the big, juicy roles, they may be forced to take on the roles of lesser characters. These represent human characteristics as real as those represented by more glamorous figures. If you have one of the more exciting parts it might be appropriate and challenging to double up and take on one of the less desirable roles. For example, if you are Connie, you may want to be Paulie too; he has a nasty role with some great lines. Sweet tonado!

3. Preparing your menu

With so many hours of movie watching ahead of you and your guests, you'll need to prepare a lot of food, and all of it Italian. Never risk not having enough

How to Recognize Michael

People will either be afraid of the responsibility for such a coveted role or they'll think they're perfect for it. Don't let personal feelings get in the way; don't choose your cousin because Michael's like your cousin. You could be Michael. Criteria for this role are different than all other roles in the movie. It's more something that swells up from the inside of the person than something that is apparent on the surface. Your Michael will be a complex person. Don't be hasty, it may take you more than one Godfather party to find him.

food. The perfect Godfather party should be a continual feast. The food should flow from start to finish and this means courses, courses, courses. There's no reason the Corleones should eat alone. Here's a suggested menu:

ANTIPASTI—Make a plate of fresh mozzarella (sliced), fresh tomatoes and basil leaves, sprinkle with a little olive oil and fresh black pepper and serve with hunks of Italian bread. Alternately, you can have fresh mozzarella and roasted peppers sprinkled with black pepper when your tomatoes are finished.
INSALATA—In a BIG bowl, the bowl you usually use for your spaghetti, mix a salad of red on-

ion, lettuce, cucumber, scallion, radish, red cabbage, green pepper, all finely chopped (when it's all in the bowl, run a knife through it) in a dressing of equal parts oil and red wine vinegar, seasoned with black pepper, salt and garlic salt. NO CREAMY ITALIAN. MAKE IT YOURSELF.

ENTREE—Spaghetti with sun-dried tomatoes and prosciutto. While your spaghetti water is boiling,

6

slice up your prosciutto and dice the tomatoes. Heat a little olive oil in a frying pan. After you throw the spaghetti in the boiling water, throw the prosciutto and tomatoes into the frying pan. After about seven minutes start tasting the spaghetti; take it out when you think it's cooked. Drain it, and add it to the prosciutto and tomatoes and sprinkle with oregano. Mix it up well and serve. Since you may be making several pounds of spaghetti, you may want to have several frying pans ready to handle the load. Never cook more than two pounds of spaghetti in one pot and figure one pound for three–four people.

**Feel free to serve any sauce you like as long as it does not come out of a jar. Selling drugs to children is not the only infamia. Avoid pesto.

POST-PASTI—This is the moment you have been waiting for, a cornucopia of pastries, tutti Italiani! Some suggestions: sfogliatelle, cannolis, rum balls, eclairs, cream puffs, eclairs, napoleons, pignoli cookies, eclairs, almond cookies.

COFFEES—Espresso is called "black coffee" by people of Italian descent. Serve it with a little piece of lemon rind in each cup. To liven up the party, serve it with a big swig of sambuca.

APERITIVO—If you serve the sambuca on the side, drop in three coffee beans. (This is considered correct. There is probably a reason for this.) You can also have anisette or anisone.

7

4. When to stop and eat

The simplest rule to follow is to eat when the Corleones eat.

This is not a smorgasbord. The courses should be served one at a time, in order. There is dignity in eating and it should never look like a free-for-all. Meals are rituals. The time when the family sits down together to eat is a time of nourishment, and not only for the body. The food is the vehicle that brings them together at the table where they talk—about each other, about love, about life, about work, about worries and concerns.

Togetherness is the key. Uncle Albert should not be in the kitchen picking at the salad while everyone else is inside eating antipasti. To facilitate this, it is perfectly acceptable to "pause" the movie while new courses are introduced.

Eating is one of the most intimate things that an Italian can do with another person. Why do we eat when we watch this movie? We eat because they are eating. We eat because we want to have a shared experience with the people in the room. But mostly, we eat because we want to have the ritual of the meal with the people in the movie.

5. Choosing your wine

Make life easy on yourself. Get a few big bottles of respectable Chianti and nobody will complain.

6. Building preparty enthusiasm

This is very important. This is the only way your guests will know that something important is going to happen. They are not just coming over on Saturday night to watch a movie; make sure they realize this. It adds to the fun and the mystery.

You can start about two weeks before calling people to talk about the menu. Find out who can bring something fresh from their neighborhood store (like bread or mozzarella) or some fresh thing from their garden (like tomatoes or basil). Include your guests in. Let them contribute. Get them excited. Ask them who they want to be. Begin to introduce the idea that this is not a passive experience. Given time, they will get into it. If *you* get into it, by the time they arrive at your home they'll be sporting black fedoras and gesticulating wildly. It's gonna be a great party.

7. Party dos and don'ts

There may not be a lot of don'ts, but the most important ones are:

DON'T TALK ABOUT ANYTHING ELSE DURING THE MOVIE. Focus. You can talk about your carburetor later.

DON'T TALK AT ALL WITHOUT PAUSING THE MOVIE. No matter how significant your comment, you don't want to miss anything, no matter how small. If it's in there, it's important.

DO PAUSE THE MOVIE FREQUENTLY. Discus-

9

sion about the film, while it's on, is encouraged and important. You and your guests should discuss how one scene relates to another, how scenes in one Godfather movie parallel scenes in another Godfather movie. Initially you talk about the obvious, like how the characters move, talk, dress. After repeated viewings your level of understanding grows, your powers of observation deepen, the things you notice become more subtle and significant. A novice will surely notice that Sonny's hotheaded; a veteran viewer will want to discuss how Sonny's famous temper actually measures up to his much quieter, but far more incitable, brother Michael.

DO SHARE YOUR DISCOVERIES. No matter how many times you watch the movie, you will always see something new. After the fifteenth viewing, Uncle Frank notices that Michael's attempt on Hyman Roth's life in the hospital in Cuba parallels the attempt on the Godfather's life that brought Michael into the family business. Share these insights with your friends and family. This is the kind of communication that enriches the Godfather experience. This is why you've invited all these people to your home.

DO WATCH SCENES OVER AGAIN IF YOU WANT OR NEED TO. Watch a scene as many times as you need to to grasp it. Don't leave questions unanswered. If you're not sure what name the Godfather calls Johnny Fontane, feel free to listen to it again and again.

8. Getting out of your role

Why bother?

9. *Incorporating* The Godfather *into your everyday life*

This is not as big a leap as it sounds. After the party, you'll find the next time you're on the phone with your cousin Sally, you slip and call him Carlo and he doesn't correct you. Pretty soon you're calling him Carlo all the time. You find yourself calling your sister Lisa "you little guinea brat," and she responds by asking "why don't you bring your whores home for dinner?" Others may not understand, but you both know that something is happening. The veil between reality and fiction is being lifted. You are not stepping into a fictional world—you are seeing the reflection of the Corleone's world in yours.

☞ O SOLE MIO *or How to Reenact a Scene from* The Godfather *When You're All by Yourself*

"Budda beep, budda bop, budda boop, budda beep." You can be Sonny whenever you want. But sometimes one line won't satisfy your urge to be in *The Godfather.* You'll crave a meatier part. There are several scenes in the movie that involve heated exchanges between two characters. You can be *both* of them. (NEVER do this when the movie is on.)

Here is a scene, complete with the props you'll need, stage direction, hand motions, and dialogue, for those of you who don't already know it.

"His Olive Oil Voice and Guinea Charm"

(Johnny Fontane and the Godfather, one desk, one chair)

[JOHNNY FONTANE SITS ON DESK, LOOKS IMPLOR-INGLY AT CHAIR] "I don't know what to do, my voice is weak, it's weak. Anyway, if I had this part in the picture, you know, it puts me right back up on top again, but this, uh, this man out there, he—he won't give it to me, the head of the studio."

[SHIFT TO CHAIR, BECOME GODFATHER] "What is his name?"

[SHIFT BACK TO DESK, BECOME JOHNNY FONTANE, LOOK DESPERATE] "Woltz. Woltz. He—he won't give it to me and, uh, he says there's no chance, no chance. [SHAKE HEAD] Months ago he bought the movie rights to this book, a bestseller, and the main character is a guy just like me. Why-uh, I wouldn't even have to act at all, just be myself. Godfather, [PUT FACE IN HANDS PATHETICALLY] I don't know what to do, [WHINE] I don't know what to do."

[SHIFT TO CHAIR, BECOME GODFATHER. LEAP UP HYS-

12

TERICALLY, GRAB JOHNNY FONTANE BY WRISTS, SHAKE VIGOROUSLY, SHOUT LINES] "You can act like a man! [SLAP JOHNNY FONTANE IN FACE] What's the matter with you? [GESTICULATE WILDLY] Is this how you turned out, a Hollywood *finocchio* that cries like a woman? [IMITATE WOMAN SOBBING] What can I do? What can I do? [GET COMPOSED] What is that nonsense? Ridiculous. [PAUSE TO CLEAR AIR] Do you spend time with your family?"

[STAND UP, BECOME JOHNNY FONTANE] "Sure I do."

[TURN AROUND, FACE YOURSELF, BECOME GODFA-THER] "Good. Because a man who doesn't spend time with his family [TURN AND GLARE AT SONNY WHO JUST WALKED IN THE DOOR] can never be a real man. [TURN BACK TO JOHNNY] Come here. [WIPE TEARS FROM JOHNNY'S FACE, PINCH HIS CHEEK, LOOK HIM UP AND DOWN] You look terrible. I want you to eat. I want you to rest well and in a month from now this Hollywood big shot's gonna give you what you want."

[TURN AROUND, BECOME JOHNNY FONTANE, MOPE] "It's too late. They start shooting in a week."

[TURN AROUND, BECOME GODFATHER, PUT ARMS ON JOHNNY FONTANE'S SHOULDERS] "I'm gonna make him an offer he can't refuse."

Here are a few other scenes that make good company when you're alone:

13

☞ The fight scene between Connie and Carlo ("You little guinea brat;" "Why don't you invite your whores home for dinner;" "Kill me, be a murderer like your father") when you're really wound up.

☞ The fight scene between Connie, Michael, and Kay after Michael has Carlo killed ("Read the paper, read the paper, that's your husband;" "Never ask me about my business"), when you feel up to being three characters.

☞ Luca Brasi practicing to see the Godfather at Connie's wedding ("Godfather, I am honored and grateful that you have invited me to your home on the wedding day of your daughter. May their first child be a masculine child"), when you don't feel like fighting.

Chapter Two

La Famiglia

☞ The Cast of Characters

VITO

"I worked my whole life . . . to take care of my family. And I refused to be a fool dancing on a string held by all those big shots. I don't apologize, that's my life."

MAMA

"Santino, I'm in the kitchen, cooking."

SANTINO

"They shot my father, it's business your ass."

FREDO

"I'm smart! Not like everybody says. I'm not dumb, I'm smart. And I want respect!"

MICHAEL

"I'm not a big shot, I'm the son of a big shot."

CONNIE

"Little guinea brat."

TOM

"He's a good lawyer. Not a Sicilian, but I think he's gonna be consigliere."

KAY

"I thought you weren't going to become a man like your father."

VINCENZO

"What happened? They threw me in a room with Joey Zasa—what's gonna happen? I bit the guy's ear off."

MARY

"Dad, why are you doing this to me?"

ANTHONY

"I will always be your son, but I will never have anything to do with your business."

☞ *Vito*

Ay, every inch a king!
—*King Lear*

Don Vito, orphaned in Sicily, narrowly escapes to America, where he marries and works in the Abbandando Groceria with Genco. Don Fanucci takes Vito's job, and Vito takes Don Fanucci's life and his neighborhood. With the help of his friends Clemenza and Tessio, the Corleone family business is born.

The founder of the Genco Olive Oil Company is a man of honor. For Vito, charity begins at home but it doesn't end there. From the beginning, he uses his influence to help people achieve justice, from Signora Colombo to Bonasera. All he asks is for a little respect, just a little bit. This Godfather is no bully. He is predictable. The people around him know what is expected of them and he understands what is expected of him.

Everything he does is for the good of his family.

☞ *Mama*

Whither thou goest, I will go
—*The Book of Ruth*

Mama is a mystery. Where does she comes from? How did she and Vito meet? What is her name?

She doesn't say a lot. She never asks where the money comes from, and she never asks Vito about his business. She's an Italian woman; she wouldn't think of it. She knows the system, she likes the system—it's her system.

She's really not mysterious at all. Vito is devoted to her (the first time we hear about her Vito is telling

17

Genco Abbandando he only has eyes for his wife); she takes care of her family; her husband is protective of her ("I don't want his mother to see him like this"); her children come to her for advice ("What did Papa think . . . . deep in his heart?"); she never loses patience with Sonny's crying kids. What else is there to know?

Only one thing. Mama cooks. A lot. Mama comes out of the kitchen long enough to sing "C'e' La Luna" at her daughter's wedding and then all but disappears. This is not because she is not an important character; it is because SHE IS COOKING. And we know that whatever she gives them to eat is very powerful food because they are very powerful men.

☞ *Santino*

**"But I will wear my heart upon my sleeve/For daws to
peck at"
—*Othello***

Sonny is the archetypal Italian man. He expresses everything he feels—and strongly. He's lusty, funny, warm, and charismatic.

Unfortunately his weaknesses are as apparent as his strengths. He's headstrong, he's fearless, he's hotheaded and he has the bad judgment to let people know. Because he's got a big mouth, the Godfather gets shot; because he is blinded by his temper, he gets killed. Sonny breaks a lot of commandments.

Unlike Michael, Sonny has a natural understanding of how the family operates, and covets his place in it. He is fiercely protective of these people because he loves them. He doesn't play at being Don—he has no ambivalence about the job, and he knows what's expected of him. His motivation is the same as the Don's but his style is more reckless. This does not make him a bad person, just a bad Don.

For all his mistakes, in spirit Sonny is the most like the Godfather.

☞ *Fredo*

"Mama used to tease me. She'd say, 'You don't belong to me, you were left on the doorstep by gypsies.' Sometimes I think it's true."

Fredo had a high fever once. This may explain why he never comes into his own in the Family. Fredo depends on the protection of his father. Sonny was always kind to him and sent him to Nevada to learn the casino business. But with Sonny dead and the Godfather gone, it's a cold, cruel world out there for Fredo.

In Michael's one trip to Nevada, he manages to

strip Fredo of whatever dignity he has acquired. He is now totally helpless and totally vulnerable and totally victimized by Michael.

Poor Fredo. Our only consolation is knowing that Michael will be tortured by the memory of Fredo's kindness for the rest of his miserable life.

☞ *Michael*

"All the perfumes of Arabia will not sweeten this little hand"
—*Macbeth*

In the boat before his death, Fredo is saying the Hail Mary. *Hail Mary, full of grace, the Lord is with thee. Blessed art thou among women, and blessed is the fruit of thy womb, Jesus. Holy Mary, Mother of God, pray for us sinners. . . .* He does not say the last line, although there is sufficient pause before Fredo is shot for Catholics in the audience to say, "Now and at the hour of our death. Amen." Bada-bing.

With this irrevocable act, Michael Corleone finally goes too far.

Michael is the central character of the movie. His drama is the central drama, his tragedy the central tragedy. He's handsome, he's brilliant, he's complex, he's brooding. And he's really mean. He doesn't crack a smile or tell a joke until he's in his fifties.

"Out, Damned Spot!"

Mentions of Fredo in Godfather III

1. *When Michael is getting his papal medal, he lapses into a memory of Fredo in the boat saying the Hail Mary before his death.*
2. *In the study during the party, Kay tells Michael that Anthony knows that he killed Fredo.*
3. *When Michael is having his diabetic stroke in the kitchen, he calls Fredo's name.*
4. *Mary asks Vinnie if Michael killed Fredo. He denies it.*
5. *Michael confesses Fredo's murder.*
6. *Connie says, "Sometimes I think of poor Fredo. Drowned. It was a terrible accident. It was God's will. But it's finished."*

Michael equivocates over everything, is as hypocritical as the sleaziest politician, is completely unable to make a decision, and has terrible judgment.

He said he would have nothing to do with his father's business, yet he ended up running it with a vengeance that would have shocked the Godfather.

He's about to kill Carlo—his sister's husband—for setting up Sonny, the killers are waiting out front, and he's asking him if he really did it. Everyone knew he did. Even Connie knew he did. But Michael needs confirmation for everything.

21

Michael Love Chart

These are the only times Michael utters the word "love" in the entire **Godfather** *saga:*

"Kay, I need you and I love you."

"It's because I admire you and I love you that I keep things secret from you." (to Tom)

"Fredo, you're my older brother and I love you."

"She was wonderful, beautiful, and I loved her." (about Apollonia)

"I love you, Kay. Don't dread me anymore."

Someone tried to murder him in his home and he didn't know whether it was Frankie Five Angels or Hyman Roth, even though Frankie tried to tell him. And Frankie is blood. But Michael has to go and quiz them about each other. Vito would have seen them coming from a mile away, and he would have known who to trust.

He promises Kay in their very first scene together that the family will be legitimate in five years. About forty years later he's still singing the same tune. Poor Michael. It seems he just keeps getting pulled back in.

He banishes his wife, kills dozens of people—friends and family, and has the cugliones to ask the dead Don Tommasino, "Why was I so feared and you so loved?" Why, indeed.

Then why can't we get enough of him?

Ever hopeful, we must think that someday Michael will get smart that he'll become the man his father was, someone we can love. After all, Vito always believed in him. He was his father's favorite. That must be why we pull for him.

Sadly, once Mary is killed, we can stop hoping. For Michael, it is over. Ah, Michael, "thou shouldst not have been old till thou hadst been wise."

Michael Joke Chart

Something drastic seems to have happened to Michael since we saw him in Godfather II. *He's killed all his enemies, he's destroyed his family, and, while a weaker man might be bowed down by his woes, Michael has developed a sense of humor. Though only one joke ever crossed his lips before,* in* Godfather III *he is constantly cracking us up.*

1. Johnny Fontane: *"Michael, where are you going? It's your favorite song!"*
   Michael: *"I'm off into the kitchen to hear some Tony Bennett records."*
2. Connie: *"Now they will fear you."*
   Michael: *"Maybe they should fear you!"*

3. Archbishop Gilday: *"In today's world, the power to absolve debt is greater than the power to forgive."*
Michael: *"Don't underestimate the power of forgiveness."*
4. Michael: *"I feel I'm getting a little wiser now."*
Kay: *"The sicker you get, the wiser you get, huh?"*
Michael: *"When I'm dead I'm gonna be really smart."*
5. Cardinal Lamberto: *"Would you like to make your Confession?"*
Michael: *"I'd use up too much of your time."*
6. Kay: *"You still have Al Neri? Why?"*
Michael: *"He helps me get in and out of the car, carries my briefcase."*
7. Michael: *"He will be appearing in . . . the opera* Cavalaria Rusticana.*"*
Anthony: *"It's* Cavalleria Rusticana, *Dad."*
Michael: *"I think I got tickets to the wrong opera. I been in New York too long."*

He's even got some of the others joking:
1. Vincent: *"Who's your father?"*
Mary: *"I'll give you a hint. He's Italian."*
2. Connie: *"Where's Mary? Would somebody please hail Mary? Sorry, Archbishop."*

When Clemenza teaches him how to shoot in The Godfather. **Watch it.**

24

☞ *Connie*

"I'd like to stay close to home now if it's all right."

In her youth, Connie made more noise than anyone else in the movie, between the shrieking, the crying, and the dish breaking. Hers is a highly coveted role at Godfather parties. The lucky person who gets to play Connie really gets to let it all hang out.

Hurricane Connie progresses from being a screamer and a fighter to a boozer and a floozie, and when she finally decides to settle down and be a matron, she poisons an old family friend with a cannoli made by the nuns.

☞ *Tom Hagen*

"He's not a wartime consigliere."

Tom is white bread. Sorry, but it's true. He might have been adopted by the Corleones, but that doesn't make him an interesting person. He starts out with some personality—he fights, he cries, he has good hand gestures. He argues with Sonny constantly because he thinks he's too wild and impetuous, yet he cries like a child when he dies and can hardly bring himself to tell the Don. He seems indifferent to Michael, yet when Michael tells him that he loves him and is leaving his family in Tom's protection, he is

A Hard Act to Follow: Being Pop's Child

"Sometimes I think I should have married a woman like you did, like Kay. Have kids, have a family, for once in my life be more . . . like Pop."
—Fredo

"It's not easy to be his son, Fredo, it's not easy."
—Michael

"I'm working for my father now, Kay."
"But you're not like him, Michael. I thought you weren't going to become a man like your father. That's what you told me."
"My father's no different from any other powerful man, any man who's responsible for other people." *—Kay and Michael*

"You're not my father!" *—Connie*

"We should all live happily for one hundred years. It would be true if my father were alive."
—Connie

"The one thing I learned from Pop was to try to think as people around you think." *—Michael*

"You were just being strong for all of us, the way Papa was, and I forgive you. Can't you forgive Fredo?" *—Connie*

"I learned many things from my father." *—Michael*

overwhelmed by emotion. And he seems to have a bit of a ruthless streak: he's pretty cool in that Nevada whorehouse.

There's not a lot more to say about him except that he loves the Godfather and is proud to be thought of as his son.

☞ Kay

"I preferred you when you were just a common mafia hood."

Really Michael—from sultry Apollonia to Kay Adams, prim New England schoolmarm?

Who *is* Kay Corleone and why do we dislike her so much? Why is she more fun to hate than a host of dangerous criminals?

Kay seems to have more in common with us than the rest of the people in the movie; she stays on the right side of the law, she's blond, and she's as American as apple pie.

But we can't hide behind Kay and tut-tut about all those nasty things the Corleones are doing. Because in reality, we're not really like her at all.

Would *you* ever wear your hair that way? Would *you* wear those tasteless clothes? And would you *ever* say such stupid things?

Since you're not as much like Kay as you'd like to believe, then you must be like the Corleones and they must be like you.

☞ *Kay Warms Up*

Kay finally moves from being pretty frosty to down-right Mediterranean by the end of the third movie. The first sign of her personality change is that she starts wearing nice clothes with warmer tones.

She has on a brown satin outfit with a nice gold blouse for Michael's party; she comes to the hospital in

Kay's Most Naive Lines

1. *"Michael, who is that scary man over there?"*
2. *"Michael, would you like me better if I were a nun?"*
3. *"I thought you weren't going to become a man like your father. That's what you told me."*
4. *"Michael, why are the drapes open?"*
5. *"There would be no way, Michael, no way you could ever forgive me, not with This Sicilian Thing that's been going on for two thousand years."*

a tan skirt suit with a pretty pin at her collar; when Michael meets her at the train station in Sicily, she is dressed in another tan suit with a high-necked shirt; and at the opera she is clad in a stunning brown velvet gown. And what hair! Kay has arrived; she looks truly beautiful. Perhaps it's got something to do with Sicily.

☞ Mary and Anthony
"Fate isn't kind to lovers."

Law or music? Against his father's wishes, the brave and defiant Anthony opts for opera and starts his career with a stunning debut in Sicily. What a rebel.

29

Kay's Ugliest Outfits

1. *At Connie's wedding, Kay wears a red polka-dot dress with a red belt and a big white collar, a big straw hat with a red band, and tasteful pearls.*
2. *Christmas shopping with Michael, Kay wears a brown chinchilla coat and a brown hat with a huge brown bow. Very festive, Kay.*
3. *When Kay foolishly tries to deliver a letter for Michael to the Mall, she wears a silly red Totes hat, red coat, and appalling black shoes. However, showing Kay in this get-up immediately after showing Apollonia—radiant and beautiful at her wedding—was a low blow.*
4. *At the Baptism, she enters her bland period wearing a simple greige dress and a hat with pink flowers. What's happening to Kay?*
5. *Kay's black-and-white striped coat sports a huge collar and huge black buttons and we get to see it twice: once, when she wants to leave the Tahoe compound (when she's also wearing a matching huge beret), and again when Michael slams the door in her face. Maybe it's the sort of coat that people don't want to be around.*

Mary is honorary chairman of the Vito Andolini Corleone Foundation, and gives away $100 million dollars her first day. What a philanthropist. Boy, are these kids removed. What connects them to the Cor-

leones is their passion—he for the opera, and she for
her father and Vincent—and their passion is their un-
doing. But otherwise, how unlike the older generation
of Corleones they are! They're sweet, they're bright,
they're really nice kids, and they're totally unfit to
run the Family Business. It's a good thing Sonny had
a way with women.

☞ *Lucy Mancini*

"Always a bridesmaid, never a bride."

Lucy was a bridesmaid at Connie's wedding, and had
six micro- mini- appearances in *The Godfather*. From
such inauspicious beginnings, who would've thought
that this seeming piece of fluff would become the
mother of the Don? And even after poor Lucy reaches
this exalted position, she still doesn't get any respect.
Three quick shots before Vincent is anybody and
she's history. In fact, she doesn't even have a name
until *The Godfather III* invests her with some
dignity.

This is every scene in which Sonny's bimbo appears:

1. At Connie's wedding, Sonny pinches her
   cheek.

2. At the dais, Sonny whispers in her ear.

31

3. Sonny's wife turns from her table to see her leaving the party with Sonny.

4. She runs up the stairs to meet Sonny.

5. She's in the bedroom with Sonny.

6. She kisses Sonny goodbye at her apartment door.

7. She arrives with Vincent at Michael's party.

8. Vincent tells her he bit Joey Zasa's ear off.

9. When Vincent is pulled into the family portrait by Michael, Lucy preens.

☞ *Vincent*

"You're the only one left in my family with my father's strength."

Vincent Mancini is the spiritual successor of his grandfather Vito. He's charismatic, powerful, and elegant. Like his father, he's tough, confident, and very warm—to say nothing of sexy. He's given making gnocchi a whole new connotation.

Vincent Mancini is a Corleone through and through. Like most of them, he feels love and hate

very strongly and it oozes out of every pore. He is loyal, and has no qualms about being pulled in to the family business.

Vinnie can't contain himself. Like Sonny, something is always moving—his hands, his body, and usually his mouth. Vinnie's "I say we make him dead" makes you downright nostalgic for Sonny's "who's head do I blow up?"

He's very much his father's son, and he's definitely the right man for the job. The Family is back on track.

☞ *Frank Pentangeli*

"Nothing in his life became him like the leaving of it."
—*Macbeth*

Who else could make "Cicci, a porte!" sound thrilling and exotic?

Frankie Five Angels is the most lovable, colorful character in the Corleone clan. He's warm and earnest and true. His voice defies description. Everything about him is perfect.

Frankie practices absolute loyalty, and is baffled and bewildered by Michael's lack of trust in him. It's through Frankie's eyes that we see most clearly the changes in the Family and in the world. Won't somebody play a tarantella for this man? He is the noblest Roman of them all.

☞ *Italian Men*

The Godfather saga gives us a panoramic view of Italianness in men.

Vito, Sonny, Clemenza, Frankie Five Angels, Johnny Fontane, Michael, Zasa, Vinnie . . . These Italian men are totally uninhibited. They indulge their every emotion: they cry, they cook, they kiss other men more than they kiss women—at least in this movie.

Genco, Nazorine, Fredo, Don Tommasino, Cardinal Lamberto . . . These Italian men belong to a slightly different school. They are gentle and kind.

34

Luca Brasi, Al Neri, Willi Cicci, Rocco Lampone . . .
These Italian men belong to a *very* different school, and
you may not want to go to that school. They may be
more violent than most people, but they're more loyal
too.

☞ *Mangiamo!*

Food, as you might expect, is a recurring feature in this
saga that is, after all, about an ordinary Italian family.
Death doesn't seem to put a crimp in anyone's appetite.
Consequently, there is eating throughout the movie.

Cooking, however, is not only a woman thing. It's
a nourishing thing, and Italian men can do it too, and
they know it doesn't compromise their masculinity.
For instance, Clemenza teaches Michael how to make
sauce, "because you'll never know when you'll need
to feed twenty guys."

The sexiest thing Vinnie does in the whole movie
is make gnocchi. This could only happen in a movie
about Italians.

Clemenza's Sauce Recipe

1. Start out with a little bit of oil

2. Fry some garlic

3. Throw in some tomatoes and tomato paste

Act Like a Man: Scenes Where Men Cry

1. Abbandando cries when he has to fire Vito to hire Fanucci's nephew.
2. Johnny Fontane cries when he can't get the part he wants.
3. Fredo cries when the Godfather gets shot.
4. The Godfather cries in bed in the hospital when Michael comes to save his life.
5. Tom cries when he tells the Godfather that Sonny was killed.
6. The Godfather cries when Tom tells him about Sonny.
7. The Godfather cries when he takes Santino to the undertaker.
8. Carlo cries before he gets killed.
9. Frankie Five Angels cries over Clemenza's death.
10. Tom cries when Michael calls him his brother.
11. Michael cries when he confesses.
12. Vinnie cries when he tells Mary he loves her.
13. Michael cries when Anthony plays the song from Corleone for him, and he remembers Apollonia.
14. Vinnie cries when he breaks up with Mary.
15. Everyone is crying outside the opera.
16. We cry when Michael dies.

Men Kissing

1. *Sonny gets Michael on the head after he volunteers to kill Sollozzo and McCluskey.*
2. *Michael and Sonny kiss before Michael kills Sollozzo and has to go to Sicily.*
3. *Michael kisses Tom at the same time.*
4. *Little Frank kisses the Godfather in bed after he comes home from the hospital.*
5. *Michael kisses Anthony goodnight after the Communion party.*
6. *Sonny kisses Michael on the head before the Godfather's surprise birthday party.*
7. *Michael kisses Fredo on New Year's Eve in Cuba.*
8. *Anthony kisses Michael in his hospital bed.*

4. Fry it, make sure it doesn't stick

5. Get it to a boil

6. Shove in all your sausage and your meatballs

7. Add a little bit of wine

8. And a little bit of sugar

And that's my trick

Chapter Three

Godfathering

☞ "That's My Family, Kay, It's Not Me" And the Rest of the Best Lines

Italians take communicating seriously. As you might expect from the people who brought you the opera, great art, and talking with your hands, their verbal skills are also highly evolved. The Corleones (and their associates) certainly have a way with words. The things they say are small works of art.

After you've watched the whole thing several times, favorite lines will emerge. Use them to spice up your speech. Be startling, be ruthless, be funny, be tough, be a Corleone.

Pick your favorite lines and say them to everyone. Assimilate.

Here are some of the best to get you started.

DON CORLEONE

"I can't remember the last time you invited me to your house for a cup of coffee." —to Bonasera, who has just asked the Godfather to kill his daughter's attackers

"And if by chance an honest man like you should make enemies, then they will become my enemies, and then they would fear you." —to Bonasera

"We're not murderers, in spite of what this undertaker says." —to Tom Hagen

"Never tell anybody outside the family what you're thinking again." —to Sonny

SONNY CORLEONE

"You gotta get up close like this—bada bing. You blow their brains all over your nice Ivy League suit." —to Michael, when he suggests killing Sollozzo

"Wadja go to college to get stupid?" —to Michael, after he enlists on Pearl Harbor day

"Save it for the liberry." —to a bodyguard who is reading a book while waiting for him to come out of Lucy's apartment

PAULIE

"Twenty, thirty grand, small bills cash in that little

40

silk purse. Marrona, if this were somebody else's wedding! Sweet tonado!" —at Connie's wedding, while eyeing her bridal purse

JACK WOLTZ
"Johnny Fontane will never get that movie. I don't care how many dago, guinea, wop, greaseball goombahs come out of the woodwork." —to Tom Hagen

CLEMENZA
"Watch out for the kids when you're backing out." —to Paulie, shortly before he gets rubbed out

"Leave the gun. Take the cannolis." —to Rocco Lampone after he exterminates Paulie

CARLO RIZZI
"Shut up and set the table." —to Connie

CONNIE
"Read the papers, read the papers, that's your husband!" —to Kay, after the Baptismal day massacre, which only Kay seems not to know about

CAPTAIN MCCLUSKEY
"How's the Italian food in this restaurant?" —to Sollozzo, shortly before they are both murdered in an Italian restaurant

CALO
"In Sicily women are more dangerous than shotguns." —to Michael, when Michael first spots Apollonia

41

MOE GREENE

"I made my bones when you were going out with cheerleaders." —to Michael

FRANK PENTANGELI

"Kid comes up to me in a white jacket, gives me a Ritz cracker and chopped liver, he says 'can o' peas.' I said, can o' peas my ass, that's a Ritz cracker and chopped liver." —to Fredo at the First Communion party

DEANNA CORLEONE

"I don't care if you are my husband, keep your greasy hands offa me." —to Fredo at the First Communion party.

"Never marry a wop. They treat their wives like shit. . . . I didn't mean to say wop. . . ." —to the guests at the First Communion

HYMAN ROTH

"I want my own doctor. Fly him in from Miami. I don't trust a doctor that can't speak English." —to his wife, after being examined by a Cuban doctor

"I'd give four million just to be able to take a piss without it hurting." —to Michael

"I loved baseball ever since Arnold Rothstein fixed the World Series in 1919." —to Michael

WILLI CICCI

"Yeah, buffer. The family had a lot of buffers." —to Senate committee hearings, when asked if there were buffers between him and Michael (watch this one; it's great.)

MICHAEL CORLEONE

"That's my family, Kay, it's not me." —at Connie's wedding, after explaining how the Godfather helped Johnny Fontane

"Keep your friends close and your enemies closer." —to Frank Pentangeli

"Don't ever takes sides with anyone against the family again." —to Fredo

"He's been dying of the same heart attack for twenty years." —to Tom, Al Neri and Rocco Lampone, about Hyman Roth

"If anything in this life is certain, if history has taught us anything, it's that you can kill anyone." —to Tom, Al Neri and Rocco Lampone

"I don't feel I have to wipe everybody out, Tom, just my enemies. That's all." —to Tom Hagen

"Am I a gangster?" —to Vincent and Joey Zasa

"If there's some guy running around this city saying

43

'fuck Michael Corleone'—what do we do with a piece of shit like that? He's a fucking dog." —to Joey Zasa

"Never let anyone know what you're thinking." —to Vinnie

"When they come, they'll come at what you love." —to Vinnie

"The higher I go, the crookeder it gets." —to Connie

VINNIE CORLEONE
"Write it in." —when told by doorman his name is not on Michael's guest list

"Say it to his face one time. Say it to his face one time." —to Joey Zasa

"I say we make him dead." —to Michael

☞ *"It's Not Personal. It's Only Business"*

The difference between business and personal is like the difference between Family and family. It's an important distinction. Whether something is business or

"I won't forget this service"

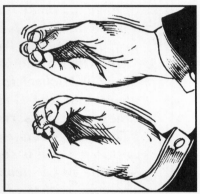

"You talk to him"

"I don't think I like what you just said"

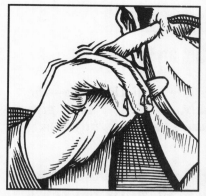

"Don't talk like that"

"Bada bing"

"What am I gonna do with you?"

I'll Make Him an Offer

The most famous line in The Godfather *saga—the Italian version of "Frankly, my dear, I don't give a damn"—appears five times in five slightly different forms:*

1. *"I'll make an offer he don't refuse, don't worry." —young Vito to Clemenza and Tessio about Don Fanucci*
2. *"I'm gonna make him an offer he can't refuse." —Godfather to Johnny Fontane about how he'll handle Jack Woltz*
3. *"My father made him an offer he couldn't refuse." —Michael to Kay at Connie's wedding, about how the Godfather broke Johnny Fontane's personal service contract*
4. *"The Turk wants to talk .... and the promise is that the deal is so good that we can't refuse." —Sonny to Clemenza, Michael, and Tom about the same deal the Godfather turned down*
5. *"I'll make him an offer he can't refuse." —Michael about buying out Moe Greene*

personal determines how you act or react, so it's critical to be able to recognize the difference. It's almost always a matter of life or death.

Since so much is riding on it, it comes up a lot in conversation.

Maxims

1. *Friendship and money, oil and water.*
2. *When they come, they'll come at what you love.*
3. *The richest man is the one with the most powerful friends.*
4. *It's dangerous to be an honest man.*

"They shot my father, it's business your ass."
—Sonny to Tom

"Tom, this is business and this man is taking it very, very personal." —Sonny to Tom, when Michael suggests killing Sollozzo

"We don't discuss business at the table." —Sonny to Carlo

"Today, I settle all family business." —Michael to Carlo

"Tell Michael it was only business, I always liked him." —Tessio to Tom

"Don't ask me about my business." —Michael to Kay

"And I said to myself, this is the business we've cho-

47

sen. I didn't ask who gave the order. Because it had nothing to do with business." —**Hyman Roth to Michael in Cuba**

"It's not personal. It's only business." —**Lucchesi to Michael in the Vatican.**

"Today the Corleone family settles its accounts." —**Vinnie**

☞ *Nine Commandments of* The Godfather

If you understand how to think Godfather, you'll un-

derstand how to talk Godfather. To begin with, they have rules. (Of course they do; they're Italian.) The rules are absolute. (Of course they are; they're Catholic.) The system is embodied in a stringent code of behavior. These guidelines to life tell the faithful what's acceptable and unacceptable. It doesn't pay to break them; look where it got Sonny.

1. Keep your friends close and your enemies closer.

2. Don't discuss business at the table.

3. Separate business from personal.

4. Don't ever take sides with anyone against the family.

5. Never interfere between a man and a woman.

6. Never tell anyone outside the family what you're thinking.

7. Keep your mouth shut and your eyes open.

8. Never hate your enemy, it affects your judgment.

9. Revenge is best when it's cold.

☞ *The* Godfather *Glossary*

Italian words resound. They have meaning beyond any literal definition. Add a tone of voice and some serious body language to these untranslatable nuances and they really sing. Why else have centuries of non-Italian speakers been able and willing to enjoy opera so much when they can't understand a word? It is not just the music. Why do so many Americans tourists in Italy understand every word their Italian-speaking cab driver says to them when he never uses a word of English? It is the desire to be understood.

The same holds true for Italian-American words and expressions. This ineffable quality of the Italian language came through Ellis Island with the people who spoke it, fused with English, and made English words resound in the same way.

**Pronunciation: In the Italian style, feel free to let go here. Don't be constrained. It's almost never necessary to say the end of a word. What is always necessary is to speak *con gusto*—emphatically and with emotion. Choose a syllable, STRESS IT, as in an-di-AAAA-mo, and swallow the rest.

Here are some words and expressions from *The God-father* that may have eluded you. Once you understand them, use them. There's nothing in English that says it better. Capisco?

ah managgia! *interjection* The verbal equivalent of biting the knuckle of your forefinger. Use it when you're annoyed or frustrated. The English equivalent is "dammit."

andiamo *verb* Let's go. In Sicilian dialect, spoken by young Vito and young Clemenza, the word is iamuninu, pronounced yamoo*neen*oo. Look for it in *Godfather II*, when they steal the rug.

aspetto *verb* Wait, just a minute, hold your horses, be quiet for one second, cool it while I straighten you out. This word is all about inflection, so increase the meaning by increasing the vehemence of your delivery. Say it this way— ash*pettt*.

bada bing *interjection* Noise that comes from a gun, and one of Sonny's favorite words. Use it only if you intend to blow someone away—that's what Sonny always meant by it!

basta *interjection* Stop, enough. This is a very functional word. Drop the phrase "say when" from your life; from here on in, it's basta. Whether it's coffee, vino or black pepper, when you've had enough, just hold up your hand and say "basta." This word also means "stop it." Use it if someone is really haranguing you. It's Italian for "I don't want to hear no more."

bella figura *adjective* Good figure, dapper. The

English equivalent is "cut a fine figure." Use it whenever you want to flatter someone who's a real dresser.

business *noun* Source of income, where the money comes from, the Family with a capital *F*. For fun, pronounce it biz*inesse*. This word goes Far beyond its ordinary English meaning to understate an enterprise that could be called an empire. Calling the Genco Import Company a business is like calling General Motors a shop.

button *noun* As in button man, hit man. "When the boss says push a button, I push a button," says Willi Cicci. This word is not likely to come up often, but can be adapted to more innocuous callings, since a button is really just the guy who does the dirty work.

caporegime *noun* The head of a subdivision of a Family.

consigliere *noun* Advisor or counselor to the Family.

draw the water from the well *idiom* Take a piece of the action, wet your beak. Use it when anyone is hogging anything, as in "You must allow me to draw the water from the well."

famiglia *noun* This is the family with a small *f*. It does not mean that it's less important; in fact, it's more important. It's the family at home; the Family is the family at work. It is a closed universe, the center of your life—and that's why "A man who doesn't spend time with his family can never be a real man," as Vito well knew.

go to the mattresses *idiom* Hide out until all is clear with the other Families. Use it whenever you're on the lam from anyone—teacher, parent, spouse.

Godfather *noun* The head of the Family. The title given to him by his friends, one of respect, one of love.

hit *verb* Kill, waste, shoot a designated person. This is what a button does.

infamia *noun* An infamy, a disgrace, a *bad* disgrace, like selling drugs to children, or molesting a little girl. This is not like being late for school or being drunk in public. These are things that shock the Godfather.

justice *noun* Fairness. An eye for an eye, a tooth for a tooth. This element of the code was central to the Godfather, who exercised it precisely. This is the first thing we learn about him—look at the opening scene with Bonasera. It escaped Michael completely, who punished every offense in the same way: bada-bing. This is one of the things that separate the good dons from the bad dons.

Mall, the *proper noun* The compound in Long Beach where the Corleones live.

marrona *interjection* Sicilian for Madonna. Roll the r's and drop the *a* and use it to express exasperation. It's the Italian equivalent of looking at the sky and saying "do you believe this?"

padrone *noun* Owner, boss, lord. Try something exotic; call your boss *padrone*. It might make her think you're afraid of her; she'll like that.

pazzo *adjective* Crazy. Pronounce it "potz" and use it indiscriminately.

pezzonovante *noun* Literally, a dollar ninety. An insulting way of referring to someone who thinks who they are. A little big shot.

sauce *noun* Short for the tomato sauce used over spaghetti. Gravy you have at home; sauce you have with other people. Sugo ("zoog") is Sicilian for sauce, as in pasta cu sugo ("pastaguzoog"), a bowl of spaghetti, and pane cu sugo ("panayguzoog"), a hunk of Italian bread dipped in sauce, in a small bowl or right out of the pot.

sleep with the fishes *idiom* Dead in the river.

soldier *noun* Gangster, common mafia hood.

stone in my shoe *idiom* Some temporary impediment, a pain in the ass.

strunz *noun* Turd. A comtemptible person. Use freely to describe anyone you don't like. The English equivalent is "shithead."

sweet tonado! *interjection* "Holy cow!"

te salud *idiom* Sicilian dialect for saying hello to or greeting someone. It makes a lovely toast. The proper Italian form is "te salute."

That Sicilian Thing *proper noun* The modern equivalent of That Ancient Roman Thing or the profane equivalent of That Sacred Roman Thing. It drives Kay to distraction.

vendetta *noun* A state of private war; getting even.

Chapter Four

We Are All
Reasonable Men

☞ *Luca Brasi Sleeps with the Fishes: Deaths and Near-Deaths, Natural or Not*

If you wanted to be cynical, you could regard the *God-father* saga as a drama that moves from one death to the next. Even Baptisms, feasts and cultural events are interrupted by what the irreverent would call rubouts.

Here is a list of every killing or serious attempt (and even some deaths by natural causes) that you'll see, excluding pain-in-the-ass innocent bystanders and people you don't know, in chronological order.

1. The murder of Vito's father, Antonio Andolini, by Don Ciccio, gets the ball rolling, even though we don't see it on screen.

2. Paolo Andolini, Vito's brother, is shot and killed by Don Ciccio's men while walking in his father's funeral procession.

3. Mama Andolini pleads with Don Ciccio for young Vito's life; when he refuses to let Vito go, she tries to stab him. She is shot and killed, but ensures Vito's escape.

4. Don Fanucci gets his throat slit by the Ninth Street boys but lives. This occurs only in the TV version.

5. Vito shoots and kills Don Fanucci in the hallway of his tenement. He fires twice and then puts the gun in his mouth and shoots again. This third shot was omitted from the TV version.

6. Back in Sicily on a visit with his family, Vito slit the throat of the man who hunted him for Don Ciccio when the Godfather was a child.

7. Also in Sicily, Vito bashes Strollo—the other man who hunted him—over the head with an oar and kills him. This occurs only in the TV version.

8. Vito slits Don Ciccio's stomach as revenge for the death of his father, brother, and mother.

9. Don Tommasino gets shot after Vito kills Don Ciccio. He escapes with a leg injury, which is why he walks with a cane in *The Godfather* and is in a wheelchair by *The Godfather III*.

10. Luca Brasi is stabbed in the hand and strangled by Bruno Tattaglia and Sollozzo.

11. The Godfather is shot five times—as Fredo looks on—and survives. It appears that Sollozzo, backed by the Tattaglia family, is responsible; when Vito gets better he tells us that Tattaglia is just a pimp and that it was Barzini all along.

12. Rocco Lampone makes his bones on Paulie with three gunshots to the head, as revenge for setting up the Godfather.

13. "We hit Bruno Tattaglia at four o'clock this morning," says Tessio to Michael. Evidently Sonny got mad.

14. Michael kills Virgil Sollozzo to prevent him from trying again to kill Vito. At the same time, he kills Capt. McCluskey, a crooked cop who got what he had coming to him.

15. Sonny gets extensively machine-gunned on the causeway, in a ruse set up by Carlo for Barzini.

16. In Sicily, where Michael is hiding out after killing Sollozzo and McCluskey, his young wife, Apollonia, gets blown up in her car by a bomb meant for Michael.

17. The Godfather dies peacefully in his garden.

18. *The Baptism Matching Column*

Rocco Lampone	Philip Tattaglia/ woman	shot in bed
Clemenza	Cuneo/Stracci	shot in elevator
Willi Cicci	Stracci/Cuneo	shot in revolving door
Unknown	Moe Greene	shot in the eye getting massage
Al Neri	Barzini and bodyguard	shot on steps of courthouse

19. Carlo gets strangled in the car by Clemenza. He kicks his feet through the windshield. "You have to answer for Santino, Carlo."

20. Tessio gets killed by Cicci, off camera, for betraying Michael.

21. We *assume* Clemenza was killed by the Rosato brothers. We know he's dead because

Frankie and Willi Cicci wear black arm-bands to Anthony's First Communion.

22. An attempt is made on Michael's life in the bedroom of his Tahoe house, "where my wife sleeps and my children come to play with their toys."

23. An attempt is made to strangle Frankie Five Angels and make him think a hit was ordered by Michael.

24. In the gunfire that ensues between the Rosato brothers and police, who break up Frankie Five Angels' strangling, Willi Cicci is shot.

25. In a setup, a Nevada prostitute meets a bloody end, leading to Senator Geary's undying allegiance to the Corleone family.

26. Johnny Ola gets strangled with a wooden hanger in a hotel in Cuba.

27. Michael's bodyguard in Miami and Cuba gets killed trying to smother Hyman Roth in the Havana hospital on New Year's Eve.

28. Mama just dies of old age. Lucky her.

29. Hyman Roth gets shot and killed by Rocco Lampone as he returns to the United States in the custody of the feds.

30. Rocco Lampone gets shot and killed by feds after he kills Hyman Roth.

31. Frank Pentangeli suffers the most interesting death in the movie. Under armed guard on an army base, he is out of Michael's reach. Since Michael can't kill him, he gets Frankie Five Angels to commit his own murder—by appealing to his honor.

32. Fredo gets shot in the head by Al Neri while Hailing Mary; sorry—while fishing.

33. Two thugs, sent by Joey Zasa to kill Vincent Mancini, get shot and killed.

34. Joey Zasa is shot and killed by Vincent Mancini on the very same street that Vito, his grandfather, killed Don Fanucci.

35. Don Tommasino gets killed in his car by the assassins hired to kill Michael.

36. The twins hired to protect Michael Corleone are both murdered at the opera, leaving Michael defenseless.

37. Don Altobello dies during the opera while eating a poison cannoli. After eighteen years, Connie finally makes her bones.

38. The Opera Matching Column

Lucchesi	stabbed in neck with eyeglasses	by Calo
Keinszig	smothered and hanged from bridge	by unknown killer
Archbishop Gilday	shot on steps	by Al Neri
Il Papa	drinks poisoned tea	by unknown killer
Calo	shot	by Lucchesi's bodyguard

39. Mary gets shot on the steps of the opera house by Mosca of Montelepre and his son.

40. Mosca of Montelepre is shot by Vincent.

41. Michael dies not-so-peacefully in his Sicilian garden.

☞ *Uh Oh!! Oh No!!*

Although fear and violence are pretty much mainstays of the movie, there are particular moments when the feeling of doom is overwhelming. The characters seem to cue us that something nasty is going to happen to someone—and it's usually them and usually because they have a big mouth.

1. "Santino, don't interfere."—Mama Corleone. "Never interfere between a man and a woman."—Don Corleone

2. "I'll have to get it myself, Pa. Paulie called in sick this morning." —Fredo to the Godfather, moments before Vito gets shot

3. "I'm an American hiding in Sicily. My name is Michele Corleone. There are people who'd pay a lot of money for that information." —Michael to Apollonia's father

4. "She's going to surprise you, she wants to drive." —Calo to Michael about Apollonia

5. "You goddamn guineas really make me laugh." —Moe Greene to Michael

6. "I don't like your kind of people. I don't like to see you come out to this clean country .... oily hair, dressed up in those silk suits and try to pass yourself off as decent Americans. I'll do business with you, but the fact is that I despise your masquerade, the dishonest way you pose yourself. Yourself and your whole fucking family." —Senator Geary to Michael at Anthony's Communion

7. "You don't know my brother Fredo, do you Johnny?" —Michael to Johnny Ola

8. "Johnny Ola told me about this place, he brought me here." —Fredo to Senator Geary

☞ *Faux Pas*

It's a serious thing to misspeak yourself. You know you've done it when it seems like everyone else in the room knows something you don't know. All eyes dart nervously around the room. People who were sitting are now standing, people who were standing are now moving, and no one is looking at you.

You will encounter the first example of this at the very beginning of the movie, when Bonasera the undertaker asks the Godfather "What shall I pay you?" to commit murder. There's a short pause, then people begin shifting nervously, eyes fly from floor to ceiling; even the Godfather stands up and puts the cat down, but no one speaks. No one can. It doesn't have words. Anyone who's ever seen an angry Italian will recognize the signs.

Bonasera has hurt the Godfather's feelings. He has misunderstood who the Godfather is and has treated him like a common hood. He has acted like the Godfather has no honor. Because this Godfather is a kind and reasonable man, once he regains his composure, he explains.

It is not only the uninitiated who can make such gaffes; close family members sometimes make the worst ones. When Sonny mouths off at the Sollozzo meeting, each and every person at that meeting shows the signs of major Italian distress. Everybody but Sonny knows what Sonny just did. Sollozzo now knows that Sonny and the Godfather disagree, and everybody there knows he knows. If the Godfather were out of the picture, Sollozzo could make a deal with Sonny. You should not be surprised when the Godfather gets shot. Clemenza, Tessio Tom, and Fredo weren't.

☞ *When Michael's Eyes Are Rolling*

If you haven't noticed already, Michael is a different kind of Don than his father. Sonny, rest in peace, may have been a bad Don, but Michael is vicious.

Unlike the general feeling of discomfort—and even fear—produced when Don Vito was angered, when Michael gets angry, something volcanic erupts inside. The music gets really loud, Michael's eyes bulge, and you know that he can hear nothing but the sound of his own rage. It's no small wonder he had a diabetic stroke.

In Louie's Restaurant in the Bronx, Michael begins

foaming when he retrieves the gun he will use to shoot
Sollozzo and McCluskey. After all, he has two good
reasons to be angry now—Sollozzo shot his father, and
McCluskey broke his jaw. By the time he reaches the
table, he is practically catatonic. His feelings find re-
lease within seconds. Bada-bing. Bada-bing. Bada-bing.

While out with Senator Geary, Michael and
"friends" in Cuba, Fredo commits his fatal "Oh No!"
when he inadvertently mentions that he pals around
with Johnny Ola after he's told Michael that he

doesn't even know him. Michael now knows that *his own brother* has set him up. Now he's really mad. He's practically reeling. He puts his hand to his head in disbelief, his eyes bulge out of their sockets, he doesn't know where to look. Watch the lady behind him; she can't take her eyes off him. He's falling into that trance again. This one will have grave consequences for Fredo.

When Michael returns from Cuba, he's pretty pumped up. When Tom tells him that Kay has lost the baby, he starts simmering. This is nothing compared to the rolling boil he reaches when Kay tells him exactly *how* she lost the baby. To make matters worse, she's not oblivious to the effect her words are having, she's *trying to get him mad.* He is going off the deep end and she rubs it in. She tells him it was a son. He is gone. His eyes roll at a new velocity. His entire face bulges. He is more mad than we've ever seen anybody. He doesn't look at her. He doesn't hear anything else she says. He just wallops her in mid-sentence. Kay will never be killed by Michael—she's his wife and the mother of his children—she'll just be put on the lay-away pain plan.

☞ *R-E-S-P-E-T-T-O*

verb *Regard with deference, esteem, or honor; avoid degrading or insulting or injuring or interfering with or interrupting, treat with consideration, refrain from offending or corrupting or tempting.*

Bold-Faced Lies

1. *"... I'm gonna wait. After the Baptism. ...
   And then I'll meet with Don Barzini and Tattaglia. All the heads of the five families."
   —Michael*
2. *"Carlo, you grew up in Nevada. When we
   make our move there, you're gonna be my
   right-hand man." —Michael*
3. *"Don't be afraid, Carlo. Come on, you think
   I'd make my sister a widow?" —Michael*
4. *"There's a car waiting for you outside. ... take
   you to the airport. I'll call your wife and tell
   her what flight you're on." —Michael to Carlo.*
5. *"No." —Michael to Kay when she asked if
   Connie's accusations about Carlo and the rest
   are true.*
6. *"I never knew no Godfather." —Frank Pentangeli to Senate committee hearing.*
7. *"You're my brother, Fredo. You don't have to
   apologize to me." —Michael*

Verb, noun, whatever. The word most often repeated in *The Godfather*.

* * *

If *The Godfather* is about anything, it's about respect. Virtually all of the drama in the movie is driven by respect or the lack of it. People get helped for having it, hated for not giving it, loved for feeling it, killed for not showing it. If you get the most of it, you're the Godfather.

Here are significant mentions:

1. "Young man, I hear you and your friends are stealing goods. But you don't even send a dress to my house. No respect! You know I've got three daughters. This is my neighborhood. You and your friends should show me some respect. You should let me wet my beak a little. I hear you and your friends cleared $600 each. Give me $200 each for your own protection, and I'll forget the insult. You young punks have to learn to respect a man like me. Otherwise, the cops will come to your house. And your family will be ruined. . . . You're a good boy. You show me respect. That's a good thing for a young man to do." —Fanucci to young Vito

2. "But, now you come to me and you say, 'Don Corleone, give me justice.' But, you don't ask with respect. You don't offer friendship. You don't even think to call me

70

Godfather. Instead you come into my house on the day my daughter is to be married and you ask me to do murder for money. . . . Bonasera, Bonasera, what have I ever done for you to treat me so disrespectfully?" —the Godfather

3. "The goddammed FBI don't respect nothin'." —Sonny

4. "Mr. Corleone is Johnny's godfather. To the Italian people that's a very religious, sacred close relationship." —Tom Hagen
"I respect that. Just tell him he should ask me anything else, but this is one favor I can't give him." —Jack Woltz

5. "I said that I would see you because I heard that you were a serious man, to be treated with respect." —the Godfather to Sollozzo

6. "Let's face it Tom, and all due respect, the Don, rest in peace, was slipping." —Sollozzo to Tom Hagen

7. "Young people don't respect anything anymore. . . . times are changing for the worse." —Don Tommasino

8. "I just came from Mr. Roth in Miami."
"How's his health?"
"Not good."

"Is there anything I can do, anything I can send?"
"He appreciates your concern, and your respect."
—Johnny Ola and Michael

9. "I'm not dumb, I'm smart! And I want respect!" —Fredo to Michael

10. "Godfather is a term that was used by his friends; one of affection, one of respect." —Michael to Senate committee hearing

11. "Joey Zasa showed up. We got him waiting in the lobby. Says he wants to personally congratulate you and show his respect." —Al Neri to Michael

12. "I have been treated this day with no respect." —Joey Zasa to the Commission

Chapter Five

Godfather Parallels

There are two possible experiences to have with *The Godfather*—the *Godfather/Godfather II* experience, and *The Godfather: The Complete Novel for Television* experience. One experience is much longer than the other, but there are other differences as well.

The differences in editing enable us to experience the Corleones in two different ways. The chronology of the television version, coupled with the addition of many intimate scenes, make the television experience more warm, human, and intelligible. We see Tom and Theresa hugging after his kidnapping; we see Sonny in the kitchen with Mama telling her that Vito has been shot; we see Michael and Kay in bed—one of the only times we see affection between them.

The effect of each is dramatically different.

THE ROMAN EMPIRE

THAT SICILIAN THING

GENCO IMPORTING

OLIVE OIL

THE CATHOLIC CHURCH

☞ *What's in the TV Version That's Not In I And II?*

1. In Sicily, Don Ciccio's men come to young Vito's house and take him and his mother to Don Ciccio.

2. In New York, young Vito sees Don Fanucci get his throat cut by the Ninth Street boys, and talks about it in the grocery with Genco.

3. Vito, Clemenza, and Tessio go to see Augustino Coppola to buy guns and listen to young Carmine play the flute.

4. Clemenza steals and sells clothes.

5. Clemenza introduces Hyman Suchowski, the future Hyman Roth, to Vito. He'll be fixing cars.

6. In Sicily, Vito kills the two men who searched for him as a child.

7. After Bonasera leaves Don Corleone's study, the Don whistles at Sonny, "Did you pay attention?"

8. After Vito tells Tom to go to Hollywood, Tom tells him that Genco, his old consigliere, is dying. The Godfather, all his sons, and Johnny Fontane go to see him in the hospital.

9. Jack Woltz gives little Janey a pony for her birthday. As Tom leaves Woltz's house, he sees Janey and her mother upstairs.

10. Connie and Carlo have a fight. When Mama tells Vito all they do is argue, he says, "Never interfere between a man and a woman." In the same conversation, he asks

Tom about Woltz and the child actress, and decides to send Luca to "reason" with him.

11. Michael and Kay, in bed in a New York hotel, call the Mall to say that they're stuck in New Hampshire and won't arrive until the next day. This is why Michael reads about Vito's shooting in the newspaper.

12. After the Godfather is shot, a detective calls Sonny to tell him. Sonny calls Tom, who's not home because he's been kidnapped.

13. Sonny tells Mama in her kitchen about Vito's shooting. He gets the Godfather's phone book from the safe, calls Tessio, tries to reach Luca, and eats a little bread. When Michael arrives, Sonny tells him not to worry, they've been through this before. A friend in the phone company calls to tell Sonny that Paulie got phone calls in the booth across the street from Genco. Sonny tries to decide whether to kill Clemenza or Paulie. Tom returns and hugs Theresa.

14. Before Clemenza, Rocco, and Paulie set out on Paulie's last ride, Clemenza shows Rocco his new car's wooden bumpers and tells Rocco that he's going to "makes his bones" on Paulie. Before Paulie is killed, Clemenza has him wait in the car while he goes into a restaurant and eats.

15. In Sicily, Michael and his guards, Fabrizzio and Calo, sit under a tree, and Michael gives himself away to the man who will later betray him.

16. Bonasera the undertaker nervously gets ready to see Don Corleone. He has no idea what service the Godfather will ask him to perform.

17. After Appolonia's death, Mike lays distraught in bed, and calls for Apollonia and Fabrizzio.

18. In the backyard of the Mall, Michael asks the Don why he hasn't avenged the deaths of Sonny and Apollonia, and tells him that his enemies will take it as a sign of weakness. In a very poignant scene, the Don tells Michael that it *is* a sign of weakness.

19. Fredo and Deanna arrive at Anthony's First Communion party fighting. During the party, Sonny's daughter asks Michael for his blessing on her engagement. When she gets it, she says, "Aunt Kay, Uncle Mike is the most wonderful man ever." Michael pores over photos of Fabrizzio, who now owns a pizzeria in Buffalo. Connie shoos Anthony from Michael's study, where he holds court.

20. The evening of the First Communion,

Frankie Five Angels and Anthony drink wine together, Al Neri kicks Meyer Klingman out of his Las Vegas hotel and Fabrizzio's car gets blown up with him in it.

21. After Fredo's death, a veiled Kay lights candles in church.

☞ *What's It All About, Francis?*

☞ Just when and how did Clemenza die? The first we hear of it is at Anthony's Communion when Fredo mentions his heart attack and points to Frankie Five Angels' black armband. Cicci tells us it wasn't a heart attack at all. Was it the Rosato brothers, Francis? Why don't we know? We've been palling around with Clemenza since the old days. Is it typical of Michael that nothing is made of this old man's death—this man who was so loyal to and loved by his father?

☞ When Frankie Five Angels goes to meet the Rosato brothers, one of them hands him a C-note on the way into the bar

What's In *I* And *II* That's Not In The TV Version?

**The Godfather *was sanitized for airing on na-
tional TV, and in the process, certain things were
lost. Here's what you missed:***

1. *After shooting Don Fanucci in the chest twice,
   Vito shoots him right in the mouth.*
2. *In Sicily, Michael walks with Apollonia and
   all her female relatives.*
3. *On their wedding night, after their first kiss,
   Apollonia takes her slip off.*
4. *Sonny's bullet-riddled body is kicked by one of
   his assassins.*
5. *Anthony receives his First Holy Communion
   in church.*
6. *Michael takes a train to Florida to see Hyman
   Roth after the attempt on his life.*
7. *In the Nevada whorehouse scene, it's a longer,
   bloodier, and more frantic scene, and features
   a good look at the dead body.*

where the meeting is to take place. When
Frankie is seated at the bar, he says this
insults him; he doesn't understand why
they gave him this money. Why did they,
Francis? Does this have any significance?

Does this have anything to do with the C-note that Frankie took from Cicci to give to Anthony at his Communion?

☞ Who is older, Sonny or Fredo? This is not as stupid a question as it sounds. In *The Godfather II*, we meet Santino by name, playing on the carpet Clemenza stole for Vito. Soon after, we see the infant Fredo sick and crying. In the TV version, first we see Fredo sick in his crib, and then we see Santino playing on the carpet. They seem to be the same age. In fact, Francis, they seem to be one and the same kid.

☞ Why is Michael staring at Enzo's cigarette lighter outside the hospital? After they save the Don's life, Enzo's hands are shaking too hard to light his own cigarette. Michael takes the lighter from his hands, lights the cigarette, and really lingers on that lighter, as if he's seen it before. Has he, Francis?

☞ What *is* the matter with Anthony, Francis?

Some things seem to have ended up on the cutting room floor of *all* versions. We're only asking.

80

☞ Not In This Movie, He Didn't

1. In *The Godfather*, during Connie and Carlo's fight, she says, "You just told me to make you dinner." Not in this movie, he didn't. In a scene in the TV version, Carlo does tell Connie to "cook him something."

2. In *The Godfather*, after Michael sees the headlines about Vito's shooting, he calls Sonny and says "Didn't Tom tell you I called?" Not in this movie, he didn't. In the TV version, Michael calls Tom earlier from Kay's hotel room.

3. In the TV version, when Michael arrives home after the Godfather's shooting Sonny says, "We been through this before with Pop." Not in this movie, he didn't. In the book, the Godfather was shot once before.

4. In *The Godfather*, after the Godfather comes home from the hospital, Tom and Sonny quarrel about revenge. Feeling that Tom is too soft, Sonny says, "Pop had Genco. I got you." Not in this movie, he didn't. In *Godfa-*

ther II, we see Genco as a young man; in the TV version we see Genco dying. But we never see Genco as consigliere.

☞ *Mistakes*

Try as you might, you're not gonna find a lot wrong with this picture. In fact, there are only three small technical errors that it may take the most seasoned repeat watcher years to catch. We'll save you the trouble.

☞ At Tom's meal with Woltz, Tom's wine glass gets filled by the waiter twice in the same few seconds of the scene—once from a front view and once from the back. And he hasn't had a sip.

☞ When Sonny beats up Carlo in the streets, he takes a swing at his face and even though we hear the punch connect, he misses by a mile.

☞ When Barzini is shot in front of the courthouse, reflected in the window of his waiting limousine is 26 Federal Plaza, which was not built until the seventies.

Miraculous Appearances

Genco appears out of nowhere in I
Frank Pentangeli appears out of nowhere in II
Altobello appears out of nowhere in III

☞ Godfather Parallels

WE'RE HAVIN' A PARTY

The Wedding	The Communion	Papal Honors
Mama sings "C'e' La Luna"		Connie sings "Eh Cumpari"
Johnny Fontane sings "I Have But One Heart"		Johnny Fontane sings "To Each His Own"
Enzo's father-in-law, Nazorine, brings in the cake		Enzo brings in the cake
FBI intruders go through parking lot and take down licenses	The police protect the parking lots	
The Godfather meets with petitioners at the wedding	Michael meets with petitioners at the Communion party	Michael meets with petitioners at his Papal Honors party
Family photo at the wedding, Kay gets pulled in		Family photo at Papal party, Vinnie gets pulled in
Vito dances with Connie		Michael dances with Mary

GODFATHER	GODFATHER II	GODFATHER III
The Wedding	The Communion	Papal Honors

WOULD IT HELP IF I SAID THEY WERE ONLY PUPPETS?

	Don Fanucci sees a puppet show at the feast before his death and says, "This is too violent for me"	In Sicily, Michael and Kay see a violent puppet show and she is disgusted by it

---

MURDER IN THE CATHEDRAL

Mass execution during the Baptism		Mass execution during the opera, which amounts to a religious ceremony

---

IF AT FIRST YOU DON'T SUCCEED

An attempt is made to kill the Godfather in the hospital	An attempt to kill Hyman Roth in the hospital	
	Hyman Roth was avenging Moe Greene's death by trying to kill Michael	Don Altobello was avenging Joey Zasa's death by trying to kill Michael

---

NEVER WAS A STORY OF MORE WOE

Apollonia caught a bomb meant for Michael		Mary catches a bullet meant for Michael

GODFATHER	GODFATHER II	GODFATHER III
The Wedding	The Communion	Papal Honors

THE APPLE DOESN'T FALL FAR FROM THE TREE

The Godfather is shot, becomes ill, and begins his decline

Michael falls ill and begins his decline

Vito says, "I swear on the lives of my grandchildren that I won't be the one to break the peace"

Michael says, "I swear on the lives of my children— give me a chance to redeem myself and I will sin no more"

The Godfather tells Michael he's too weak to avenge Sonny and Apollonia's deaths, but lets Michael do it

Michael tells Vincent that he no longer has the strength to kill his enemies, and makes Vincent the Don so he can do it

The Godfather is told by Michael, "I'll handle it. I told you I can handle it, I'll handle it"

Michael is told by Vinnie, "Give me the order and I'll take care of it"

After rising from his chair to play with his grandchild, Vito dies in his

Michael dies alone in a chair in his Sicilian garden fruitful garden

GODFATHER	GODFATHER II	GODFATHER III
The Wedding	The Communion	Papal Honors

HE PUT IN HIS THUMB AND PULLED OUT A PLUM

A gun is hidden behind the WC in Louie's Restaurant in the Bronx for Michael to kill Sollozzo and McCluskey	A gun is hidden in a chimney on a tenement rooftop for Vito to kill Don Fanucci	It looked like there would be a gun hidden in Lucchesi's office for Calo to kill him with, but there wasn't

THE VOICELESS WAILING

Woltz screams when he finds Khartoum's head in his bed		Michael screams a chilling scream when Mary is killed

I'M BEGINNING TO SEE THE LIGHT

	Michael has a heart-to-heart with Mama about losing his family	Michael has a heart-to-heart with Don Tommasino's corpse about not being loved

THREE-CARD VITO: THE PUPPETEER AND NOT THE PUPPET

Johnny Fontane wants out of his personal service contract. The Godfather begins by offering Johnny's bandleader $10,000		

GODFATHER	GODFATHER II	GODFATHER III
The Wedding	**The Communion**	**Papal Honors**
to let him go, and ends up paying $1000	Signora Colombo's landlord tries to evict her. Vito begins by offering him an increase in rent, and ends up getting the rent cut by ten dollars a month, and the dog stays	
	Fanucci asks Vito for $600. Vito begins by offering $100, and ends up stealing all the money out of Fanucci's wallet	
	Senator Geary tries to shake Michael down for $250,000. Michael begins by refusing to pay the full amount Geary asks for a gaming license, and ends up making Geary pay for it	

DON'T CALL ME, I'LL CALL YOU

Michael tells Clemenza and Tessio "I have plans," and that they're going to have to wait to start their own families	Michael tells Frankie "I have business with Hyman Roth, I don't want it disturbed" and that Frankie has to wait to sort out his problems with the Rosato brothers

GODFATHER	GODFATHER II	GODFATHER III
The Wedding	**The Communion**	**Papal Honors**

FRUIT SALAD

Michael is decorated with what Vito calls "Christmas ribbons" in the war		Michael is decorated by the Pope

WHAT'S A NICE GIRL LIKE YOU

Kay asks Michael, "Who is that scary man over there?" about Luca Brasi		Grace Hamilton, the photographer at Michael's party, says to Vinnie, "Look at that spooky-looking guy," about Joey Zasa's bodyguard

THE BELLA FIGURA AND THE FEAST*

	Vito kills the dapper bully Don Fanucci at the Feast	Vinnie kills the dapper bully Joey Zasa at the Feast

*The two festival street scenes are exactly the same, right down to the Santucci street sign next store to the Abbandando Groceria.

CHEF OF THE FUTURE

Clemenza makes sauce		Vinnie makes gnocchi

GODFATHER	GODFATHER II	GODFATHER III
The Wedding	**The Communion**	**Papal Honors**

ET TU, FRUITE

Vito stops and buys oranges from a vendor just before he's shot	Young Vito stops and buys oranges from a vendor	
	Michael eats an orange while planning the murder of Hyman Roth, Fredo, and Frankie Five Angels with Tom and Al	Vinnie plays with an orange when they're at Don Tommasino's house
The Godfather is eating an orange when he dies		Michael dies and an orange rolls off his lap onto the grass

STRANGE BEDFELLOWS

The Godfather wants Michael to become a senator	Michael says to Senator Geary, "We're both part of the same hypocrisy"	Michael wants Anthony to be a lawyer

BORN YESTERDAY

Vito tells Luca to pretend to go over the Tattaglia family		Michael tells Vinnie to "betray" him to Altobello

91

GODFATHER	GODFATHER II	GODFATHER III
The Wedding	**The Communion**	**Papal Honors**

THE KING IS DEAD, LONG LIVE THE KING

Al Neri and Clemenza kiss Michael's hand and declare him Godfather		Al Neri and Calo kiss Vinnie's hand and declare him Godfather

IS THIS THE THANKS I GET?

Michael takes Sollozzo out and Vito thinks it's wrong		Vinnie takes Joey Zasa out and Michael thinks it's wrong

I'LL HAVE MY GIRL CALL YOUR GIRL

The Dons meet to discuss drug trafficking	The power brokers meet in Cuba	The Commission meets in Atlantic City

EVERY PARTY HAS A POOPER

When Michael arrives at the party in Las Vegas, he kicks the girls out, and Fredo tells the band to leave		When Michael arrives at the Commission meeting in Atlantic City, the girls leave, and the band stops playing

Chapter Six

The Godfather Road Map

What follows is a scene-by-scene tour of *The Godfather, The Godfather II, The Godfather: The Complete Novel for Television,* and *The Godfather III.*

You've probably already noticed that scenes appear in a different sequence in the television version than they did in the original two movies: while *The Godfather* and *The Godfather II* move back and forth in time from the movie's present to the near and far past, *The Complete Novel for Television* is in chronological order, beginning with Don Vito Corleone's youth in Sicily. *The Godfather III* picks up where these earlier movies both leave off.

Use this as a guide to find your favorite scene, your favorite line, your favorite character. It will help you out in any Godfather emergency.

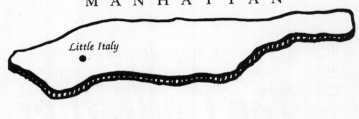

MANHATTAN

Little Italy

SICILY

● *Corleone*

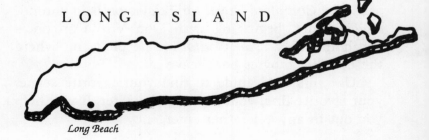

LONG ISLAND

Long Beach

WHERE THEY LIVE

94

The Godfather

New York

Bonaserarriva is in the Godfather's library asking for justice for his daughter

Connie and Carlo's wedding is going on outside

Vito walks away from the family photo because Michael's not there

Shots of Godfather and Mama, Connie and Carlo, FBI looking at license plates, Clemenza dancing, Tessio eating

Barzini arrives at the wedding

Paulie thinks about what's in Connie's wedding purse

A photographer tries to take a photo of Barzini

Luca Brasi practices his thank-you speech to the Godfather

Sonny yells at the FBI, then breaks a photographer's camera

In the library, the baker asks for help keeping Enzo, his future son-in-law, from being deported

Michael and Kay arrive and dance

Luca continues rehearsing

Michael and Kay eat, Tom comes over to talk to them

Luca goes in to see the Godfather

Connie and Carlo dance

Sonny makes his move on Lucy Mancini

Mama sings while Sonny and Lucy dash upstairs

Johnny Fontane arrives and sings, Vito goes outside to watch

Godfather hugs Johnny after he sings, then takes him inside

Fredo introduces himself to Kay

Johnny tells the Godfather he wants a part in a movie

The wedding cake is marched in

Godfather tells Tom to go to California

The family photo is taken, with Kay

Godfather and Connie dance

Tom goes to Woltz's studio in Hollywood

Tom and Woltz at dinner

Shot of mansion, Woltz finds horse's head in bed with him and screams

Vito, Sonny, and Tom talk about the upcoming Sollozzo meeting

The Sollozzo meeting

Luca gets ready to go see the Tattaglias

Michael and Kay Christmas shop at Best & Co.

Luca is killed

Tom is taken by Sollozzo

The Godfather gets shot while Fredo looks on

Coming out of Radio City with Michael, Kay sees newspaper headline about Vito

Clemenza goes to Sonny's, who sends him to get Paulie

Sollozzo calls Sonny about Tom

Tom and Sollozzo talk

Michael arrives

They're told that Luca is dead, Sonny orders hit on Paulie

Paulie drives Clemenza and Rocco to city

Paulie killed on the way back to Long Beach

Kay calls Michael while Clemenza makes sauce

Michael has dinner with Kay in hotel room

Michael visits Vito in the hospital, Enzo helps saves Vito

Capt. McCluskey breaks Michael's jaw

Bada-bing scene: Michael decides to kill Sollozzo

Clemenza teaches Michael how to shoot

The boys eat Chinese while waiting for Michael's dinner with Sollozzo

Michael in the car with Sollozzo and McCluskey on the way to Louie's Restaurant in the Bronx

Michael kills Sollozzo and McCluskey

The men hit the mattresses; shots of New York newspaper headlines

The Godfather comes home from the hospital

Tom and Sonny argue about revenge for the Godfather shooting

Sicily

Walking to Corleone, Michael meets Don Tommasino, who warns him that he's not safe

GIs drive by

Michael sees Apollonia, sits at her father's bar

Dinner with Apollonia's family

Michael, Apollonia, and family go courting

New York

Sonny leaves Lucy Mancini's apartment, picks up Connie, who's been beaten up by Carlo

Sonny beats Carlo up

Sicily

Michael marries Apollonia

She undresses and he kisses her in their bedroom

New York

Kay turns up at the Mall with a letter for Michael

The Connie/Carlo fight scene

Sonny goes to help, gets shot on the causeway and kicked by gunman

Tom tells Vito about Sonny's death

The Godfather at the funeral parlor with Sonny

Sicily

Michael teaches Apollonia to drive

Don Tommasino tells Michael about Sonny, and that it's become too dangerous for him in Sicily

Michael tells Fabrizzio to get his car

Apollonia is killed when the car explodes

New York

The Godfather makes peace at a meeting with the heads of all the families

In the car, Vito tells Tom that Barzini is responsible for everything

Michael goes to New Hampshire to see Kay and proposes

Clemenza and Tessio ask for their own territory

Carlo is told he'll be Michael's right-hand man in Nevada

Tom is farmed out, sent to Nevada

Michael goes to Vegas to see Moe Greene where Johnny Fontane signs contract to appear in hotels; Moe Greene won't sell out

Back in New York, Kay tells Michael that Connie wants him to be the baby's godfather

Vito warns Michael that a traitor will try to set up a meeting

The Godfather dies

At the funeral, Tessio sets up the meeting

The Baptism: Philip Tattaglia, Cuneo, Stracci, Barzini, and Greene are all killed

Tessio's meeting is called off and Tessio is killed

Michael confronts Carlo about Sonny and Carlo is killed

In front of Kay, Connie accuses Michael of killing Carlo

Al Neri, Rocco Lampone, and Clemenza kiss Michael's hand

THE GODFATHER, PART II

Sicily

Vito Andolini's father's funeral procession

Shots are fired, young Vito's brother Paolo is killed

At Don Ciccio's house, Vito's mother begs for the boy's life and is killed

Don Ciccio's men search the town for Vito

Vito is hidden as men continue to search

Vito aboard ship from Italy passing Statue of Liberty in New York

New York, past

On Ellis Island, Vito Andolini is renamed "Corleone" and quarantined with smallpox

Vito looks out his window at the Statue of Liberty

Tahoe

Inside church in Nevada, Anthony Corleone makes his First Communion

Anthony's First Communion party

Connie and Merle Johnson arrive

Senator Geary gives a speech, the choir sings

In the study, Geary tries to shake down Michael for a casino license

Frankie Pentangeli eats canapes

Johnny Ola meets with Michael

Frankie tries to get the band to play the "Tarantella"

In Michael's study, Connie asks for money

The family eats together in the evening of the Communion party

Deanna falls down and fights with Fredo

Frankie and Michael talk about the Rosato brothers

Michael and Kay dance

Shots are fired through Michael and Kay's bedroom window

Chase outside for assassins

Michael turns things over to Tom while he's gone

Deanna finds the bodies of the would-be assassins

Michael is kissing Anthony good-night after the party, before he leaves for Florida and Cuba

New York, past

In his apartment, Vito holds his baby

Vito is at theatre with Genco Abbandando, a player sings "Mama"

Don Fanucci walks out in the middle of the show

Vito and Genco go backstage

Fanucci threatens the theatre owner and his daughter

Outside, Genco explains the Black Hand to Vito

At dinner one night, Clemenza throws guns through Vito's window for him to hide

Fanucci comes into the groceria to get a job for his nephew

Vito is fired

On the street, Abbandando offers Vito a box of groceries, which he refuses

Vito goes home, leaves a pear on his wife's plate and kisses her

Vito meets Clemenza on street

At a cafe, Clemenza offers Vito a rug in thanks

Clemenza and Vito steal the rug and carry it home

A crying Santino plays on the new rug

Florida/Cuba

In Florida, Michael drives to Roth's house; they talk in the living room

In New York, Michael visits Frank Pentangeli

Johnny Ola calls Fredo in the middle of the night

Frankie is strangled, Cicci is shot

Tom arrives by airplane in Nevada to meet Fredo; Tom with hysterical Geary and bloody body of prostitute in Nevada whorehouse

Back in Tahoe, Kay is stopped from leaving compound

Michael drives through Cuba, sees children begging

Michael meets with Roth and government officials and investors

Michael sees killing of rebel in street

At Roth's birthday party, he looks for Michael's $2 million

Fredo arrives with the money

Fredo and Michael sit at an outdoor restaurant, Michael tells Fredo he's planning to kill Roth

Michael meets Roth again in his hotel room

Geary, Fredo, Ola, Michael and others see a show at a Cuban casino

At a sex show, Fredo slips up about knowing Johnny Ola

Ola is strangled

New Year's Eve party in Cuban President's mansion

Attempt on Roth's life in Cuban hospital

Soldiers enter New Year's party, Michael kisses Fredo

Wild street scene as President resigns

Michael escapes, and tries to take Fredo with him

Michael returns to Tahoe and meets with Tom, who tells him Kay has had a miscarriage

New York, past

Fredo has pneumonia

Vito drives a truckload of dresses, Don Fanucci gets in the truck and threatens him

At dinner with Clemenza and Tessio, Vito plans to kill Fanucci

At the Feast, Vito gets $50 from Clemenza and Tessio to bring to Fanucci

At a café, Vito gives Fanucci $100, and wipes cheek where Fanucci pinched it

Fanucci goes to the Feast while Vito climbs across tenement roofs

Fanucci watches a puppet show

Vito retrieves a gun hidden on the roof, waits in Fanucci's hallway, and loosens a light bulb as Fanucci comes up the stairs

A priest blesses the crowd at the Feast

Vito shoots Fanucci once, and shoots again as fire-works go off and then he shoots him in the mouth

Back on the roof, Vito breaks up the gun, takes his money from Fanucci's wallet, and goes back to the Feast

Vito sits with his wife and three children on his stoop and tells the infant Michael he loves him

Tahoe

Michael arrives home, Kay is sewing; they don't talk

Willi Cicci testifies in Washington

Michael and Mama talk about losing his family

New York, past

A fruit-stall owner gives Vito free oranges

At home, a widow with a dog comes for Vito's help with her landlord

Vito sees the landlord in the barber shop and talks to him in the street about the widow

Next day, the landlord comes to see Vito, abashed

The Genco Import Co. sign goes up

Tahoe

Michael testifies in Washington; Geary gives support-ive speech

Frank Pentangeli with the feds on an army base

Michael and Tom talk about Frankie

Michael has it out with Fredo and cuts him off; orders Neri not to kill Fredo while Mama's alive

Frankie is taken to testify, sees his brother sitting with Michael, and refuses to talk

In the Hotel Washington, Kay tells Michael she's leaving him

Sicily, past

Vito and family get off the train and drive to Don Tommasino's house

Dinner al fresco, with a shot of small Santino and Fredo

The family visits a winery

Vito drives to Don Ciccio's house with Don Tommasino

Vito stabs Don Ciccio to death, and Don Tommasino shct in leg

The family in Corleone square with a priest

Their train pulls out of the station as they leave Sicily

Tahoe

Mama dies

At Mama's wake, Fredo and Connie hug and Fredo asks Tom if he can see Michael

Connie intercedes with Michael for Fredo, and asks him if she can stay home and take care of him

Michael sees Fredo

Tom, Michael, and Neri talk about Roth; Tom is given his orders

Fredo and Anthony go fishing

Tom goes to see Frankie

Connie tries to slip Kay out of house before Michael sees her; he slams the door in her face

Connie calls Anthony in from fishing with Fredo

Roth is arrested at airport

Feds yell to Frankie, who's taking a bath

Roth is shot at the airport

Frank Pentangeli is found dead

Fredo is shot as Michael looks on

Michael remembers Fredo's kindness on Pearl Harbor Day (Vito's birthday) and remembers being with Vito on the train leaving Sicily; he sits on a chair outdoors and thinks

THE GODFATHER: THE COMPLETE NOVEL FOR TELEVISION

Sicily

Vito Andolini's father's funeral procession

Shots are fired, young Vito's brother Paolo is killed

Don Ciccio's men come to take Vito from his mother

At Don Ciccio's house, Vito's mother begs for the boy's life and is killed

Don Ciccio's men search the town for Vito

Vito is hidden as men continue to search

Vito aboard ship from Italy passing Statue of Liberty in New York

New York

On Ellis Island, Vito Andolini is renamed "Corleone" and quarantined with smallpox

Vito looks out his window at the Statue of Liberty

New York, later

A mature Vito delivers groceries

Vito is at theatre with Genco Abbandando, a player sings "Mama"

Don Fanucci walks out in the middle of the show

Vito and Genco go backstage

Fanucci threatens the theatre owner and his daughter

Outside, Genco explains the Black Hand to Vito

In his apartment, Vito holds his baby

Back at work, Vito sees Fanucci get his throat slit

In the Abbandando Groceria, Genco tells Vito about what happened to Fanucci

Vito goes home, leaves a pear on his wife's plate and kisses her

Fredo has pneumonia

Fanucci comes into the groceria to get a job for his nephew

Vito is fired

On the street, Abbandando offers Vito a box of groceries, which he refuses

At dinner that night, Clemenza throws guns through Vito's window for him to hide

Vito meets Clemenza on street

At a cafe, Clemenza offers Vito a rug in thanks

Clemenza and Vito steal the rug and carry it home

A crying Santino plays on the new rug

Clemenza, Tessio, and Vito meet Augustino Coppola at his workshop; Carmine Coppola, a child, plays the flute for them

Clemenza steals clothes, and sells them to housewives

Vito drives a truckload of dresses, Don Fanucci gets in the truck and threatens him

At dinner table with Clemenza and Tessio, Vito plans to kill Fanucci

At the Feast, Vito gets $50 from Clemenza and Tessio to bring to Fanucci

At a café, Vito gives Fanucci $100, and wipes cheek where Fanucci pinched it

Fanucci goes to the Feast while Vito climbs across tenement roofs

Fanucci watches a puppet show

Vito retrieves a gun hidden on the roof, waits in Fanucci's hallway, and loosens a light bulb as Fanucci comes up the stairs

A priest blesses the crowd at Feast

Vito shoots Fanucci once, and shoots again as fireworks go off

Back on the roof, Vito breaks up the gun, takes his money from Fanucci's wallet, and goes back to the Feast

Vito sits with his wife and three children on his stoop and tells the infant Michael he loves him

A fruit-stall owner gives Vito free oranges

At home, a widow with a dog comes for Vito's help with her landlord

Vito sees the landlord in the barber shop and talks to him in the street about the widow

Next day, the landlord comes to see Vito, abashed

Clemenza introduces Vito to Hyman Suchowski, who'll fix cars, and changes his name to Hyman Rothstein

The Genco Import Co. sign goes up

Sicily

Vito and family get off the train and drive to Don Tommasino's house

Dinner al fresco, with a shot of small Santino and Fredo

Vito sneaks inside and kills a man who hunted him as a child

Later, he finds Strollo, the other man who hunted him, in a rowboat, and beats him with an oar

The family visits a winery

Vito drives to Don Ciccio's house with Don Tommasino

Vito stabs Don Ciccio to death, and Don Tommasino is shot in leg

The family in Corleone square with a priest

Their train pulls out of the station as they leave Sicily

Long Beach

Bonasera is in an older Godfather's library asking for justice for his daughter (Vito whistles at Sonny to get his attention)

Connie and Carlo's wedding is going on outside

Vito walks away from the family photo because Michael's not there

Shots of Godfather and Mama, Connie and Carlo, FBI looking at license plates, Clemenza dancing, Tessio eating

Barzini arrives at the wedding

Paulie thinks about what's in Connie's wedding purse

A photographer tries to take a photo of Barzini

Luca Brasi practices his thank-you speech to the Godfather

Sonny yells at the FBI, then breaks a photographer's camera

In the library, the baker asks for help keeping Enzo, his future son-in-law, from being deported

Michael and Kay arrive and dance

Luca continues rehearsing

Michael and Kay eat, Tom comes over to talk to them

Luca goes in to see the Godfather

Connie and Carlo dance

Sonny makes his move on Lucy Mancini

Mama sings while Sonny and Lucy dash upstairs

Johnny Fontane arrives and sings, Vito goes outside to watch

Godfather hugs Johnny after he sings, then takes him inside

Fredo introduces himself to Kay

Johnny tells the Godfather he wants a part in a movie

The wedding cake is marched in

Godfather tells Tom to go to California, Tom tells Vito that Genco is dying

The family photo is taken, with Kay

Godfather and Connie dance

Father, sons, and Johnny go to the hospital to see Genco

Vito takes Michael aside before going to Genco's room, is bitter about his attitude

Genco asks Godfather to frighten away death

Tom goes to Woltz's studio in Hollywood

Woltz is giving child star Janey a pony for her birthday

Tom and Woltz at dinner

Leaving the mansion, Tom sees Janey and her mother leaning over the banister

Back in Long Beach, Connie and Carlo argue and Mama tells Vito, Sonny and Tom; Vito says not to interfere

Vito asks Tom about Woltz and the little girl; they decide to send Luca to "reason" with Woltz

Shot of mansion, Woltz finds horse's head in bed with him and screams

Vito, Sonny, and Tom talk about the upcoming Sollozzo meeting

The Sollozzo meeting

Luca gets ready to go see the Tattaglias

Michael and Kay Christmas shop at Best & Co.

Michael and Kay in bed in a hotel

Luca is killed

Tom is taken by Sollozzo

The Godfather gets shot while Fredo looks on

A detective calls Sonny, Sonny calls Tom

Coming out of Radio City with Michael, Kay sees newspaper headline about Vito

Clemenza goes to Sonny's, who sends him to get Paulie

Sollozzo calls Sonny about Tom

Sonny joins Mama in the kitchen and tells her about the shooting

Sonny calls Tessio after getting Vito's phone book from his safe

Tom and Sollozzo talk

Michael arrives, Sonny mentions an earlier shooting

A phone company connection calls Sonny

Sonny and Tessio discuss whether to kill Paulie or Clemenza

Tom returns

They're told that Luca is dead, Sonny orders hit on Paulie

Paulie drives Clemenza and Rocco to city; they pull into a parking lot, Clemenza goes into restaurant and eats

Paulie killed on the way back to Long Beach

Kay calls Michael while Clemenza makes sauce

Michael has dinner with Kay in hotel room

Michael visits Vito in the hospital, Enzo helps saves Vito

Capt. McCluskey breaks Michael's jaw

Bada-bing scene: Michael decides to kill Sollozzo

Clemenza teaches Michael how to shoot

The boys eat Chinese while waiting for Michael's dinner with Sollozzo

Michael in the car with Sollozzo and McCluskey on the way to Louie's Restaurant in the Bronx

Michael kills Sollozzo and McCluskey

The men hit the mattresses; shots of New York newspaper headlines

The Godfather comes home from the hospital

Tom and Sonny argue about revenge for the Godfather shooting

Sicily

Walking to Corleone, Michael meets Don Tommasino, who warns him that he's not safe

Michael sits under a tree talking with Fabrizzio and Calo

114

Michael goes to the village square in Corleone
GIs drive by
Michael sees Apollonia, sits at her father's bar
Dinner with Apollonia's family

New York

Sonny leaves Lucy Mancini's apartment, picks up Connie, who's been beaten up by Carlo
Sonny beats Carlo up
Kay turns up at the Mall with a letter for Michael

Sicily

Michael marries Apollonia, kisses her in their bedroom

New York

The Connie/Carlo fight scene
Sonny goes to help, gets shot on the causeway
Tom tells Vito about Sonny's death and calls Bonasera
Bonasera, frightened, waits for the Godfather to arrive
The Godfather at the funeral parlor with Sonny

Sicily

Michael teaches Apollonia to drive
Don Tommasino tells Michael about Sonny, and that it's become too dangerous for him in Sicily

Michael tells Fabrizzio to get his car

Apollonia is killed when the car explodes

Michael is in bed, delirious

New York

The Godfather makes peace at a meeting with the heads of all the families

In the car, Vito tells Tom that Barzini is responsible for everything

Godfather and Michael make plans in the backyard; Michael asks him why he's not avenging Sonny and Apollonia, and says Vito gave his word but he didn't give his

Michael goes to New Hampshire to see Kay and proposes

Clemenza and Tessio ask for their own territory

Carlo is told he'll be Michael's right-hand man in Nevada

Tom is farmed out, sent to Nevada

Michael goes to Vegas to see Moe Greene where Johnny Fontane signs contract to appear in hotels; Moe Greene won't sell out

Back in New York, Kay tells Michael that Connie wants him to be the baby's godfather

Vito warns Michael that a traitor will try to set up a meeting

The Godfather dies

At the funeral, Tessio sets up the meeting

The Baptism: Philip Tattaglia, Cuneo, Stracci, Barzini, and Greene are all killed

Tessio's meeting is called off and Tessio is killed

Michael confronts Carlo about Sonny and Carlo is killed

In front of Kay, Connie accuses Michael of killing Carlo

Al Neri, Rocco Lampone, and Clemenza kiss Michael's hand

Tahoe

Anthony's First Communion party

Fredo and his wife arrive, Connie and Merle Johnson arrive

Frank Pentangeli eats canapes

In the study, Sonny's daughter asks Michael's blessing on her engagement

Michael looks at photos of Fabrizzio

Frankie tries to get the band to play the "Tarantella"

In Michael's study, Connie asks for money

Johnny Ola meets with Michael

Connie chases Anthony from house

Senator Geary gives a speech, the choir sings

In the study, Geary tries to shake down Michael for a casino license

The family eats together on the evening of the Communion party

Deanna falls down and fights with Fredo

Frankie and Michael talk about the Rosato brothers

Frankie and Anthony drink wine

Michael and Kay dance

Al Neri forces Klingman out of his Vegas hotel

Fabrizzio's death

Michael is kissing Anthony good-night after the party, before he leaves for Florida and Cuba

Shots are fired through Michael and Kay's bedroom window

Chase outside for assassins

Michael turns things over to Tom while he's gone

Deanna finds the bodies of the would-be assassins

In Florida, Michael drives to Roth's house; they talk in the living room

In New York, Michael visits Frankie

Johnny Ola calls Fredo in the middle of the night

Frankie is strangled, Cicci is shot

Tom and Fredo with Geary and dead prostitute in Nevada whorehouse

Back in Tahoe, Kay is stopped from leaving compound

Florida/Cuba

Michael drives through Cuba, sees children begging

Michael meets with Roth and government officials and investors

Michael sees killing of rebel in street

At Roth's birthday party, he looks for Michael's $2 million

Fredo arrives with the money

Fredo and Michael sit at an outdoor restaurant, Michael tells Fredo he's planning to kill Roth

Michael meets Roth again in his hotel room

Geary, Fredo, Ola, Michael and others see a show at a Cuban casino

At a sex show, Fredo slips up about knowing Johnny Ola

Ola is strangled

New Year's Eve party in Cuban President's mansion

Attempt on Roth's life in Cuban hospital

Soldiers enter New Year's party, Michael kisses Fredo

Wild street scene as President resigns

Michael escapes, and tries to take Fredo with him

Michael returns to Tahoe and meets with Tom, who tells him Kay has had a miscarriage

Michael arrives home, Kay is sewing; they don't talk

Tahoe

Willi Cicci testifies in Washington

Michael and Mama talk about losing his family

Michael testifies in Washington; Geary gives supportive speech

Frank Pentangeli with the feds on an army base

Michael and Tom talk about Frankie

Michael has it out with Fredo and cuts him off; orders Neri not to kill Fredo while Mama's alive

Frankie is taken to testify, sees his brother sitting with Michael, and refuses to talk

In the Hotel Washington, Kay tells Michael she's leaving him

Mama dies

At Mama's wake, Fredo and Connie hug and Fredo asks Tom if he can see Michael

Connie intercedes with Michael for Fredo, and asks him if she can stay home and take care of him

Michael sees Fredo

Tom, Michael, and Neri talk about Roth; Tom is given his orders

Fredo and Anthony go fishing

Tom goes to see Frankie

Connie tries to slip Kay out of house before Michael sees her; he slams the door in her face

Connie calls Anthony in from fishing with Fredo

Roth is arrested at airport

Feds yell to Frankie, who's taking a bath

Roth is shot at the airport

Frank Pentangeli is found dead

Fredo is shot as Michael looks on

Michael remembers Fredo's kindness on Pearl Harbor Day (Vito's birthday) and remembers being with Vito on the train leaving Sicily; he sits on a chair outdoors and thinks

THE GODFATHER, PART III

With scenes of the sadly neglected house in Tahoe in the background, Michael writes to Mary and Anthony asking them to his ceremony of Papal Honors, and to ask their mother to come as well

In a New York church, Michael receives the Honor of St. Sebastian for his charitable work. Kay arrives as the ceremony ends

Connie sings "Eh Cumpari" with Dominic Abbandando at the party at Michael's house that follows

Vincent Mancini, Sonny's illegitimate son, arrives at the party, uninvited, and forces his way in

Scenes from the party: Joey Zasa arrives singing, Don Altobello greets Kay, Dominic Abbandando talks to the press

Mary introduces herself to her cousin Vinnie

Connie makes a joke about hailing Mary

Mary gives a speech and hands a huge check to Archbishop Gilday, as honorary chairman of the Vito Andolini Corleone Foundation

Johnny Fontane sings "To Each His Own"

Michael and Kay have a hostile meeting before joining Anthony in the study to talk about his career

More party scenes: Grace Hamilton meets Vinnie, Michael introduces Father Andrew Hagen to the Archbishop, Grace introduces herself to Michael

Al Neri tells Michael that Joey Zasa wants to see him

Michael gets a plaque from Zasa; Connie brings Vincent in and he and Zasa argue

The family photo is taken, with Vincent

Enzo the baker brings in the cake

Michael and Mary dance to a toast of "cent'anni"

At Vinnie's apartment, he kills two thugs sent by Zasa

Michael chastises Vinnie for the killings

Michael meets with Archbishop Gilday, the head of the Vatican bank in Rome and offers to buy Immobiliare

The Immobiliare board approves Michael, subject to Vatican ratification

During a meeting in Michael's car, Don Altobello tells Michael that his old partners want to be a part of the legitimate Immobiliare deal, and agrees to set up a meeting

In Vatican City, Lucchesi and Keinszig block Michael's approval

In a café downtown, Mary asks Vinnie about Fredo

Vinnie and Michael discuss Zasa in a helicopter over Atlantic City

The Commission meeting gets rubbed out "the old Don's way"

Michael has a diabetic stroke in his kitchen and is rushed to hospital

B.J. Harrison goes to see Archbishop Gilday to tell him Michael is sick, but the Immobiliare deal must go through

Connie gives Vinnie and Al the order to hit Zasa

Kay and his children visit Michael in the hospital and they tell him that Anthony will debut in Sicily

Mary and Vinnie make gnocchi at Vinnie's club

Vinnie kills Zasa at the Feast

At the hospital, Michael yells at Connie, Neri, and

Vinnie for hitting Zasa, and warns Vinnie away from Mary because "they'll come at what you love"

Michael and Don Altobello promise to see each other in Sicily

Sicily

Michael, Vinnie, and Mary arrive in Sicily to a rousing welcome

Michael and Vincent meet with Don Tommasino, who tells them that Lucchesi is the Vatican/Commission connection

At a luncheon to celebrate his debut, Anthony sings and Michael has an Apollonia flashback

Michael takes a walk with Mary and Anthony, and tells Mary she can't see Vinnie anymore

Vincent and Mary listen to Elvis in the bedroom

Vincent shaves Michael, who tells him to go sell himself to Don Altobello

Vincent meets with Don Altobello and then Lucchesi

Don Tommasino and Michael go to see Lamberto to tell him Michael's being swindled; Michael makes his Confession

Pope Paul VI dies

Connie gives Michael his insulin shot on the veranda, and he tells her about going to Confession

Don Altobello goes to see Mosca of Montelepre to set up Michael's assassination

Kay arrives in Sicily and is met by Michael, Mary, and Connie

Mosca and his son prepare for the hit

Vincent and the twins, Michael's bodyguards, play pool

Kay and Michael tour Sicily

Connie talks to Vincent in the pool room and tells him she wants revenge if anything happens to Michael

Michael and Kay see a puppet show in Corleone square

Mosca kills Don Tommasino and his driver

Kay and Michael have lunch at Don Tommasino's house while waiting for him to return

Calo tells Michael that Don Tommasino is dead

Everybody votes for Pope and Lamberto wins, becoming John Paul I

Keinszig goes missing

Archbishop Gilday tells Keinszig on the phone that the new Pope "has very different ideas"

Michael keeps a vigil with the body of Don Tommasino

Vincent tells Michael an assassin has been hired to kill him; Michael steps down because he "can't do it anymore" and agrees to let Vinnie kill all his enemies before they kill him

Vinnie becomes Don Corleone on condition that he give up Mary; Calo, Al Neri, and Vinnie's sidekick kiss his hand

The crowd arrives at the opera house; the twins stand guard

At a reception inside, Connie gives Altobello a special cannoli

Vinnie breaks up with Mary

The opera begins

Neri boards a train to the Vatican

Altobello begins eating his cannoli

Calo arrives at Lucchesi's house

Mosca kills the first twin

Calo gets frisked by Lucchesi's bodyguards

Neri, on the train, looks at his gun hidden in a box of candy

In the opera, Turiddu bites Alfio's ear and Vinnie grins

Mosca kills the other twin

The Pope is brought his tea

Keinszig gets "a message from Vincenzo Corleone"

The Pope is found dead

Don Altobello finishes off his cannoli and gets finished off

Neri kills Archbishop Gilday

Calo kills Lucchesi with his eyeglasses and Calo gets killed

Keinszig swings from a bridge in London

The opera ends

Mary is shot on the steps of the opera house; Michael screams

Michael flashes back to dancing with Mary at his party, dancing with Apollonia at their wedding, dancing with Kay at the First Communion, then dies a lonely old man

☞ Miscellaneous

☞ Whose phone number is Long Beach 4-5620? This is the number that Michael calls from the Godfather's hospital room. At first blush, it appears to be the Godfather's number, but it's more likely to be Sonny's. Sonny has been taking the family calls since the Godfather's shooting; Sonny would be the one Michael would call for help.

☞ Whose number is OR9-9539? This is the number that Michael and Kay call from the hotel at Christmas to say that they won't be there until the next day. It seems to be either Tom's number, or the Godfather's number.

☞ Who sings "Have Yourself a Merry Little

HOW TO PICK A FIGHT

Christmas" when Michael and Kay are outside of Best & Co. after Christmas shopping? (Johnny Fontane)

☞ What is the Godfather's birthday? (December 7)

☞ What are the seven days of the week according to Apollonia? (Monday, Tuesday, Thursday, Wednesday, Friday, Sunday, Saturday)

☞ What is Virgil Sollozzo's nickname? (The Turk)

☞ What is the number of the Godfather's house? (110)

☞ Why are Sonny's kids always crying? When we see Sonny as a baby, he's crying, too.

☞ Does the scene in the back of the car with the Godfather and Tom look familiar? Is it shades of *On the Waterfront*?

☞ What football game was Hyman Roth watching when Michael came to visit? (Notre Dame vs. USC)

☞ How many of the seven sacraments do we see in *The Godfather I, II, and III*?
(Four: Connie and Carlo are married and their baby is baptized, Anthony has his First Holy Communion, and Michael goes to Confession. Two other sacraments made peripheral appearances: Andrew Hagen, Tom's son, becomes a priest, having received Holy Orders, and the hospital room scene between the Godfather and Genco is a sort of secular Extreme Unction. In the book, Connie and Carlo's son receives Confirmation, the seventh sacrament.)

129

☞ What was Kay eating at Connie's wedding? (Lasagna)

☞ What was Sonny eating with the Godfather and Tom Hagen before the Sollozzo meeting? (Peanuts in shells)

☞ What did Don Corleone have in his mouth when he died? (A slice of orange)

☞ What was Mama cooking when the Godfather came home from the hospital? (Chicken cacciatore)